CHANGE !T UP

CHANGE !T UP

The "Get Real, Get Happy"
Guide That Just Might Help You Succeed
Where Others Have Failed

By
Karen Judd Smith
Marilyn Morris

www.TheSolutionRevolution.co

GDG
PRESS

DEDICATION

To our beloved family, friends and colleagues who endured hearing us exclaim, "We're getting there, not quite, but almost!" and especially Kevin, who having heard that phrase ad infinitum, kindly offered to read and edit for us yet again…one more time.

Contents

Introduction

What? Another Self-Help Book That Promises To Really Help? Yep!

Why, why, oh why are we writing this book? Have we always been fascinated by the self-help genre? Nope. The resources for this book are derived from just about everything but that. Did we study marketing and then design a product we thought might make a million bucks? Nope, again. We're pretty realistic about this. We just hope the contents of this book are as helpful to others as it has been for ourselves, as well as those we have (overtly and covertly) helped turn from pained frowns into small smiles, even a guffaw here and there.

Activating people's innate creative, solutions-building juices is, quite simply, a great deal of fun. Helping them consciously, intentionally deal with their knotty problems and watching them derive the benefits sooner than they imagined possible is even more fulfilling!

Do we have some kind of burning desire to help people delve down into the mire of their existence by interpreting the deeper meanings of their dreams? No, no, no. Sure, we've taken our share of psychology and related courses and appreciate the basic concepts, and it's all quite interesting, but dream therapy? Nah.

As for our graduate and post-graduate education, one of us studied physics and the other comparative religions. We both have Theology degrees (that's how we met) and one of us has two of them. One never became a pastor and instead got involved in United Nations work. That one also managed a fleet of boats, restructured a bus charter & tour company, completed her doctoral program in international peace and justice and is currently a board member and consultant for several non-profits and NGOs (non-governmental organizations at the UN).

The other did become a pastor, became tired of endless committee meetings, ventured into health care and is currently a hospice chaplain. She also writes and publishes short stories, poetry, and her own musical compositions.

How then did we get to this point of co-writing a self-help book on approaching life with a problem free mindset? And what do we mean when we say, "problem free" anyway? Simply put, we mean a life where you become clear about who you really are and what you really want.

We mean a life where you innovate and invigorate your conversations and relationships with confidence. We mean a life in which you engage in meaningful "PLAY." And yes, we mean this both literally and figuratively. We explain this acronym more fully later, but here is a preview version:

Pause (breathe deeply to reconnect with your body)
Lean in (Don't fight the moment. Do **L**ook for exceptions and examples)
Adapt (now aware, **A**djust to this context)

EnjoY!—(celebrate what you have achieved, no matter how small)

The co-authors of this book are a lot like you. We're professional people with busy personal lives, and a bit on the self-motivated side. As such, we have ventured down the self-help trail ourselves, more than once, when confronting some of our more difficult problems.

What we found, to our surprise, because we somewhat trusted the "experts" (though were less impressed with them over time), is that most self-help programs are, well, less than helpful. Often there's just too much touting of the self-help guru, along with a lot of motivational "rah, rah," without sufficient, real, down-to-brass-tacks, "how-to."

Now, if you resonate with that assessment, this could be a very fun, and yes, seriously helpful little guide for you. We try not to "rah, rah," for one, and second, we spend as much time as possible on real, "how-to."

Self-help is a huge industry in America. We are a culture that thinks of itself as a nation of sturdy folks who can pull themselves up by their bootstraps. So, here you are looking for more insight and leverage on one or more problems in your life and you've found our little book.

Allow us to clarify for whom this book is likely to work best, and you can see if you fit into one of these categories:

1) Anyone with a problem who really wants to deal with it comprehensively.

2) Anyone with a problem who hasn't quite yet decided they want to deal with it, but is thinking they should maybe get around to it.

3) Anyone with a problem.

The cool thing about this book is that you are going to learn some handy techniques that have been tried and proven to work in clinical and non-clinical settings over several decades. Even cooler is that these techniques apply to any problem, every problem.

Too good to be true?

Not really. If you think about it, all problems are simply puzzles we haven't figured out. This book will make no attempt to educate you about your *specific* problems, but it will help you become a good puzzle solver.

To be frank, even blunt, (and we're not being unkind here), we don't care so much as to what your problem is, how it came into your life, who brought it there or all the reasons why it seemingly won't go away.

Of course, we are fully aware of how problems are often painful. We know this, as we've suffered through many a problem ourselves. But this book isn't about how to more comprehensively understand your problem. Rather it only focuses on one thing, and that is, how to discover and implement your own solutions, tailor made, for each and every problem you want to deal with.

We can't do anything about problems you don't want to move beyond, but we can surely guide you on what to do when it comes to taking on the ones you want to resolve. And, you may want to continue looking for information and advice about your particular problem. No shortage of that exists.

Need to lose weight, find faith, repair your marriage, understand your teenager, get rich quick without much effort, prevent war or secure world peace? Somewhere, an author, radio or TV host, journalist, preacher, guru, life coach, professor, financial advisor, etc., is out there, deeply wanting, very willing, and all too expertly eager to tell you more and more and more about your problem.

Most are sincerely dedicated to helping you overcome your problem, although there are some who just want your money and care nothing about your success (they're too busy securing their own).

However, and this is unfortunate, many self-help programs employ what we call the #1 BIG Mistake (see chapter one) that ultimately prevents them from being truly helpful.

Before we go further, let us impart one important warning: the self-help in this book isn't terribly difficult to understand. Nor is it all that hard to do.

It does not require you to meditate deeply on the meaning of life. Neither do you need to reach for the highest peaks of personal insight. You won't need to stoke "fire in the belly" motivation in order to conquer your fears, shore up your will power, or keep yourself in a training mode for an Olympic-sized effort. But you will need to do something!

That's right. This isn't the hardest self-motivated program, but neither is it tailor made for couch potatoes waiting for their fairy godmother to wave her magic wand over them and make all the bad things go away. After all, self-help implies that you want to at least *do* something to improve your lot.

So, here's our handshake with you: If you can commit to taking one small step at a time, and not in any particular order, only in whatever order you choose is best for you, then we guarantee you success, even if you do some of the steps wrong.

We hope you take this rather easy-to-do deal, not because we want to sell a book; rather, we know you can really have some fun with what we have to share, and you just might learn some truly helpful things along the way.

In case you need a bit more convincing, we're going to share with you our own personal experience of learning and practicing these techniques you're hopefully about to learn. And yes, it is humbling to share some of the vulnerable parts of our lives, as well as others' lives.

Not every example is going to be taken from a profoundly difficult problem, though some examples will. The point is that your problems are unique to you and whether it's a serious problem, or just a simple thing that perplexes you from time to time, we do believe this approach will help you.

As you move through the book, you will note interjections from both authors, Karen and Marilyn. There's a reason for that. It's how the book evolved, starting as a conversation that lasted several years and eventually distilled into what you now hold in your hand.

So, there will be comments from each of us, some from Karen's perspective as the developer, teacher and coach of the system introduced in this book (the Solutions Mastery Matrix & System), and some from Marilyn's experience as a student and practitioner of that same system.

We begin with Marilyn's reminiscence of a mid-life crisis, when she was outwardly successful, climbing up the corporate ladder, but quietly dying inside, living anything but an authentic, meaningful life on her own terms.

It was in the midst of several impending life-challenging storms when she sought for a way to deal with problems that was efficient and effective. She had tried several other methods and was fed up with what she felt were more or less, "pie-in-the-sky" approaches.

Marilyn's Story

A few years ago, when I was desperately trying to keep my life from falling apart (and not succeeding), I needed something I could use while on the fly, running between a full-time professional career and full-time personal life, both filled with extensive obligations.

I had been fulfilling so many expectations from others that I had seriously neglected my own needs, to the point where I was deeply suffering—intellectually, emotionally, even physically.

Here's a list to show you how comprehensive the problem areas in my life were:

1) Marriage coming to an end
2) Weight gain out of control
3) Health issues related to weight gain
4) Bad boss making an otherwise good job miserable
5) Exhaustion from dealing with miserable job
6) Teenagers acting out at home and at school
7) Emotional ups and downs, a la, "menopause"
8) Financial pressures from the housing bubble that gutted our bank account and hobbled our credit

I felt as if I had nowhere to turn for help. I felt that my problems were too heavy for friends, and certainly did not want to show any chink in my armor to colleagues at work or fellow churchgoers. Besides, none of these resources seemed effective to me. I had tried before to unburden my cares with friends and co-congregates, but all they could do was give me well-intentioned, but not very applicable, advice.

Believe me, I understand how it feels to hear people give you advice that you know you can never follow. Nothing is more downright annoying, or worse, deeply discouraging. You wonder, "what the *bleep* is wrong with me? How come they can do all that, and I can't?"

Another resource that also felt completely inapplicable were those late night TV self-help gurus who invented the infomercial genre. You know the kind.

I would come home after a long shift at the hospital, turn on the TV to wind down, and inevitably, this all too enthusiastic king of the self-help realm would appear with his huge grin, filled with equally huge shiny white teeth, to encourage me to find and follow my passion. Ugh. I had nothing left for passion!

Perhaps he has helped a lot of people become successful. I haven't a clue, but he always made me feel awful about my state of affairs. Had I found my passion? Would I follow it if I had? Was I motivated enough to achieve phenomenal success? If not, then I needed to buy his books and sign up for his seminars, and then do this, that, and all the other. His elongated ads only left me more exhausted.

Again, all well and good to those for whom his program works. But, let me reassure you, really, really reassure you, that's not what's being proposed here. When I say the content of this book works for the average person, I mean it. I'm not rich or famous, not even close.

I may have the benefit of higher education, but let me be honest about that in context of the guidance provided here. While I greatly appreciate what I learned in college and graduate school, the bulk of that education was how to research and understand the history of something, how it started, evolved and arrived at its current state.

Maintaining problems is hugely expensive, whether at the individual level or in complex international entanglements.

In essence, much of my higher education prepared me to work in the corporate world, where I have spent much of my adult life "drilling down" on problems in order to solve them. While problem-oriented applications can be useful, what I began to notice (quite painfully) was that when I would use these same strategies in my personal life, things only got worse!

My conundrum was this: the more I tried to analyze and understand my problems, the more deeply entrenched those problems became! It was becoming unbearable.

What that says for corporate America, you can surmise for yourself. But, I will say that corporations, governments, heck, even the United Nations are not doing as good a job as they could when it comes to solving problems with an expedient use of time and resources. Maintaining problems is hugely expensive, whether at the individual level or in complex international entanglements.

In the midst of all this mess, I decided I needed a serious break and scheduled a 2-week vacation, the first I had given myself in more than 20 years. I used that time to visit an old friend from seminary days, the co-author of this book.

Not long into that visit, in the midst of catching up, I discovered that she had already embarked upon a journey of profound self-reinvention in a way that I had longed to do, but had never quite figured out how to do. I swallowed some pride (okay, I humbled myself big time) and asked her what was helping her get through similar upheavals in life with a lot less, well, upheaval.

She then shared with me her exploration into some well-established techniques that have been proven effective over a long period of time and with thousands of clients from all socio-economic backgrounds. She had already put together many components to what would become her "Solutions Mastery System," and was beginning to teach others how to use them.

I have to admit, I was battle fatigued and wary of anything supposedly new, so my initial approach was very cautious, and at one point, I flat out rejected some of the concepts. But, recall that list above. Guess what? It got worse! My health took a plummet that led to short-term disability and unemployment.

If there was ever a time in my life to throw up my hands in despair, then was it. But also, if there was ever a time to test if any of what Karen had developed really did work, then was also a golden opportunity.

So, I started. It went slow at first. I had a few intellectual hurdles to make, a few concept adjustments to incorporate. Nothing was hard to understand, per se, but a few mental habits had to be dealt with.

Once I made those tweaks, however, I began to notice immediate effects, good ones! The results weren't fantastic at first, just small things that seemed better. But, as I continued, things got even better, and then even better still. The work isn't over—after all, neither is my life—but positive outcomes have indeed happened, and at a surprisingly steady pace.

You've read the "before" list above. Here's my "after" list—that is, after testing out and then consistently practicing Karen's Solutions Mastery System:

1) Marriage ended amicably
2) Weight gain turned into weight loss
3) Health issues significantly lessened
4) A great job in an enviable weather zone
5) Emotional & physical well being much improved
6) The kids are doing all right!
7) No "pause" after "meno" … life goes on!
8) Finances resolved with payments we can handle

I am deeply indebted to Karen, not only as a friend, but also as an adept life coach, who has spent an enormous amount of time (days, weeks, months, years) to develop this system that guides me, and could guide you to achieve the life that you really want (and not just what you think others expect of you).

The Solutions Mastery System

We have experienced how wonderful it is to successfully re-engage and re-invigorate our lives through the use of the tools provided in the Solutions Mastery System, in particular, its core component, The Solutions Matrix (which we refer to as "the Matrix"). The diagram of the Matrix below is not complicated, consisting of only 5 components, each a line of inquiry that helps you find solutions to your problems, fast!

This book will explain exactly how to use this neat little tool that is so concise it could fit in your pocket. (Look for a link to a printable PDF in the Resources section).

EXPLORING   EXCEPTIONS

MQ

EVALUATING   EXAMPLES

Just as with anything newly learned, becoming skillful with the Matrix is an ongoing process. But you will start to naturally want to make it your new default approach to solving problems. It's more fun than just about any other problem solving strategy we've ever tried. We hope you find it as much fun, too.

The system provides you with a quick and easy way to notice when you're caught in a "doom and gloom" or DAG loop (more in the glossary), and how to escape those self-created black holes. You know those self-fulfilling prophesies in which we allow our problematic circumstances to rule our thinking, so much so that we "see" our failure coming, and then, huh, not so surprisingly... we produce that outcome!

So rather than just tell you what you "shouldn't do" and leave you floundering to figure out what you to do, we share with you a fun 2-minute JumpStart exercise that will help you fire up the clusters of thought so you start that journey to *your desired emotional, psychological, physical, personal, professional destination,* quick-smart!

Don't get us wrong. We're never going to tell you what *you* want. That part is totally up to you. We too have had our share of trips and falls, and with them, our measure of tears. But, using the Matrix has re-engaged us with the "magic" of life, the fun of being surprised, but not overwhelmed by whatever it presents us.

The secret of all this is that we are actually providing you with simple, totally doable retraining steps that give you the power to choose the direction you want to pursue, and then no longer to be tossed willy-nilly by the prevailing circumstances of any particular day.

For example, take new findings in Neuroscience about how the conscious part of our brains function. We like to think that we are mostly driven by our will power and persistence.

We say to ourselves, "I want to lose weight. I'm going to get fit. I'm going to make more money. I'm going to find the love of my life." We then think, "If I only apply enough will power and persistence, I can achieve that desire."

However, science shows that these and other similar conscious efforts represent only 2% - 4% of our thought patterns and behavior. Only 2% - 4%!

That's why a lot of those self-help programs don't work. They are designed to motivate you to greater use of will power and persistence. But these alone are simply not adequate.

You could consider our system as an antidote to self-help, given what self-help has usually been about up to now. Our system is designed to circumvent heavy reliance on either will power or persistence. It is a gentle, step by simple step system that addresses the issue of how the majority of our actions (and therefore our "results" (happiness, success, etc.) are largely shaped by our subconscious brain.

This area, the larger part of what drives us in our daily lives is currently called, "implicit memory systems." It's a highly efficient part of us, when you think about it. So much of what we do is "automatic;" otherwise, we'd be spending all our time re-thinking how to tie our shoes, drive a car, or interact with family, friends and colleagues.

However, the subconscious does not filter what's good or bad for us. It just stores what we learn over time, and then prods us to "wash, rinse, repeat." Problems arise when our "wash, rinse, repeat" cycles are no longer helpful, and worse, become harmful.

Learning and maintaining new cycles is hard for this reason. We feel "weak" in the beginning of any new endeavor because we haven't developed the mental muscle for it. That's why so many resolutions are sabotaged within days or weeks after we make them.

Our system breaks down that learning into small, doable, easy steps that you design yourself, for yourself. Even if you do your steps out of order, or some other way "wrong," it won't matter much, and we'll explain why. In fact, the "wrong" way just might be the right way for you.

There are other reasons why the Solutions Mastery System works and works extremely well. First, it is based on practices that have been proven in clinical studies for decades now, backed up and enhanced by neurological research.

We could explain in depth about those clinical studies (we did include a good sample of the academic literature on them in the resource section). But, neither you nor we have to be mechanics to learn how to drive a car. Karen studied the genre in depth because she wanted to distill it into a teachable format for the average person, i.e., people like her friend Marilyn, who is not a rocket scientist.

We do want you to have the essential "how to" information so that you can use the Matrix when you need it, in the same way you access your phone's GPS with a few taps and swipes or voice instructions.

Again, you don't need to know programming to use the GPS, or any app for that matter. You just need to know how to use it, and then apply it, as in the way you use the GPS to locate a nearby restaurant. Metaphorically, we won't promise you intergalactic travel, though. After all, in reality, not even the GPS can teleport you anywhere–yet!

As you become familiar with this Solutions System and its Matrix, getting yourself underway with the GPS when needed, when the emotional fogs roll in, you won't run aground. You will continue to move forward with a growing confidence because you have a proven track to run on—a system you know that works.

This system works for moms, dads, teens, software engineers, entrepreneurs, interior designers, movie stars, farmers, politicians and scientists, rocket or otherwise. Why do we have confidence to say that? We've seen it work for us, and those whom we've taught, and they represent all of, and more than, the above.

The "PLAY" (pause, lean in, adapt, enjoy!) aspect of the Solutions System puts you squarely at the helm of what happens each step of the way. Because it is a system, when you are at a loss, perhaps not feeling confident, or worse, hit a really rough emotional patch, you can use just 2 minutes of PLAY to get yourself back on track. Hopefully, we will someday hear about your successes (our website information can also be found in the resource section).

Disclaimer (and look, not in fine print): This book contains information suitable for self-help. If you have serious medical and/or psychological problems that need professional attention, by no means should you substitute anything advised in this book for the guidance received from appropriate professionals.

This includes, but is not limited to, support groups, psychologists, doctors, lawyers, financial planners and other appropriate professional counsel. Please seek out the above if you feel you have signs of ongoing depression, or have harmful thoughts toward yourself or others, or need legal advice of any kind, or are experiencing physical symptoms that need a doctor's attention.

We intend to complement, not substitute for, the helping professions. Further, nothing in this book is intended to counter or alter your personal or religious beliefs, nor dissuade you from any political, moral or ethical perspective you may already hold. What we address is specific to approaching and applying common sense techniques toward problem solving, nothing less, nothing more. (Isn't that helpful enough?).

Consider the "big ideas" and "essential questions" of this system as something of a gasoline additive, designed to clear your engine from grungy old concepts so that your "life-engine" runs cleaner, faster, better, longer. Feel free to continue using whatever regular fuel (philosophy, religious affiliation, political views, professional help, etc.), you already have, so long as it doesn't hurt you or anyone else.

One thing we sincerely hope is that you have some fun, even a lot of fun, with our self-help system. In our experience, even the stickiest problems melt away faster when we are able to add a little levity in the midst of creating solutions.

This system really does help you with that too. How? Well, with the benefit of the system's insights, if you are able to step back for a moment from the utter seriousness of your circumstances to see how strangely unhelpful you are being to yourself, and then begin to realize how easily it can be fixed–you just might LOL!

We have had the healthy benefit of such moments. They felt good, terrific, liberating! And that's why, we promise you that we will do our best to help you come to those moments as well.

The Stories

One final note on the "boxed stories" we have put in gray boxes throughout the book. Co-authoring a book has many a joy and, we discovered, raised additional questions, such as, "Whose voice do we write this in?"

To include both voices, we have included comments throughout from both of us. Plus we have added snippets of others' stories, ones we heard directly, and paraphrased them as best as possible. So they are our writing, their story. We hope those asides help to illustrate how practical and down-to earth is the magic of the Matrix!

Part I:
CHANGING THE
CONVERSATION

1. What the World (and each one of us) Needs Now

and it's not just "Love, Sweet Love"

The difficulties and challenges that arise in our lives show us at least one thing: we never quite arrive at that place in life where we know everything. Surprising, huh?

Problems, difficulties, bad situations, complications, headaches, issues, obstacles, questions, puzzles, roadblocks, logjams—whatever phrases we use, simply indicate some kind of learning still needs to take place. Sometimes a little. Sometimes a lot. Unless we prefer things to stay as they are.

One seriously unfortunate facet of most of the list of words above, and the feelings we recall as we replay the problem scenarios to which we attach those words, is that they are laden with hopelessness rather than opportunity.

Already, we are presented right here with at least three main options: First, give up, because the (insert any word from above list) is just too hard. Second, change our words and hopefully somewhat alter our stories. Third, change our words, *and* get excited that we have an opportunity to challenge our old concepts and thus create new ones!

Before you wrinkle your nose that we said those oft used buzz words, "opportunity" and "challenge," you might want to recall those teenage years when you thought it was a blast to *choose* to do exactly the opposite of what one of the major gods of your life (mom, dad, sibling, teacher, coach, anyone else) was telling you (not) to do! Challenges were once, and can yet again be fun!

For those for whom the word, "No" has little meaning, problems are opportunities in the disguise of a challenge. As for the rest of us, we don't often think of problems as helpful. But they actually are, when we take the time to consider them from another angle, and that is what we intend to help you do in this book.

For those for whom the word, "No" has little meaning, problems are opportunities in the disguise of a challenge.

A problem makes more apparent what it is that we have to deal with (what we have yet to do to get to the other side of the issue). There is nothing inherently "unfixable" about problems at all. What makes a problem almighty may be related to several things aside from the problem itself, such as indecision within the person confronting the problem.

Indecision is perhaps the paramount issue when dealing with problems, though there are other factors. What we hope to help you do is initiate and manage good decisions, lots of them, starting with little decisions that then add up to bigger decisions.

These decisions will get you through those days when you feel stumped, stymied, confused, unable, overwhelmed, or even when you might be in a bit of danger of some kind.

Of course, others might look on and advise, "Hey, why don't you tackle that problem in this way?" But they aren't *you*! What we're going to emphasize in this book, several times, is that you have all you need within you to handle your toughest problems.

We're going to show you how to use exceptions, examples, evaluating and exploring skills that will help you create and craft successful solutions.

Problems are not omnipotent, omniscient or endless. They may have a name, perhaps a face, a shape, a color or smell. But noticing a problem is good. Really. Honest! Because, if you don't notice there's a problem, you won't have the motivation to find a solution. And that leaves people around you frustrated and angry that you're oblivious to something that clearly isn't quite right.

What if there were some simple ways to tackle each and every problem? What if we didn't have to get a Ph.D. about any particular problem in order to solve it? Wouldn't that make our problems less daunting?

Think about this. When you were little and got your first pair of tennis shoes, you were presented with a problem. You looked up at your mom or dad and wondered, "What do I do with these loose strings here?" You had to learn some simple twists and turns, and after a few days of practice, voila! Problem solved. Shoe tied. Go play.

That's exactly what we want to provide for you here. A few simple steps we know will guide you around, over or under whatever it is that has you sinking in your personal quagmire, the thing you have labeled "problem."

Don't worry. You won't need to sift through a dictionary or thesaurus to understand the steps we're going to guide you through. We've done all that for you.

We've sifted through quite a bit of academic and clinical work. As we learned it, we then distilled it further into simpler language and easier to follow steps, so that others could quickly learn it and practice it on their own.

Notice Your Reactions,
The Stories You Are Telling Yourself

Changing our conversation, the way we talk to ourselves, and to others, about problems is the essential step toward solving any of those problems. If we cling to the same old "impossible" words about problems, it becomes very difficult to engage anything new toward resolving those problems.

That's why conflicts drag on and on, between neighbors, married couples, different cultures and nations at odds. When people and groups, usually motivated by exhaustion, change their language about the problem, their impasse begins to crack open. Resolution can happen, and does happen, as history shows us over and over, but never without first a change in conversation.

In the very next chapter, we're going to give you one mind-blowing concept that will help you begin to change your conversations about problems, _forever_.

We can all get our heads around the idea that a problem is an opportunity. We've heard it so often at work that we respond almost reflexively with, "yeah, yeah, yeah, blah, blah, blah." Even so, redefining problems as opportunities does make intellectual, logical sense.

The hard part is getting our hearts around the idea that when presented with a problem, we could actually feel grateful ... because problems are personal, and they hurt. We are humans, emotional beings that feel first, then react to those feelings with a thought process.

We don't mean we should be grateful about problems in a facetious way. However, when we confront a problem, we can, and should, take a moment (a few slow, deep breaths) and allow ourselves to have a sliver of hope, if not gratitude, that if we can see that something isn't right, we can also find a way to make it a little more right, if not altogether right!

Now in all truth, if you could find an alternative fast-track way to solve your problems that feeling of gratitude would come a bit easier, wouldn't it? And that's what we discovered, a way to fast-track out of the slow muck of problems and the rapid fluid of creative solutions.

It's almost as good as magic. No, it's better than magic, because magic is nothing more than a clever illusion. But the lines of inquiry we go over in the next few chapters are very real. They are succinct questions that help you create doable solutions for your stickiest problems.

If you get through those chapters and still prefer to call on some fairy godmother to come to the rescue, we won't begrudge that tactic, if it works for you. In fact, if she's real, and truly effective, send her number to us!

What we *are* saying here is that solving your problem could be easier than you think. We understand that problems are painful, and often loom so large as to seem impossible. But, we also know, from the techniques we've employed in this book, that each and every one of us can do something, at least one small thing, here and there, to solve a problem, any problem, no matter how big and complicated it may have become. Those small actions can lead to eyebrow raising results.

Life-changing conversations then, are the ones that are transactional, exchanging or adding some new information, perhaps even adding skills or using interpersonal muscle that we haven't flexed before.

For the simple steps we will outline to make the most sense to you, we will be asking you to do a little self-reflection and some personal inquiry. But, we won't be asking you to go back through your past and blame yourself, or others, and wallow around in how bad your problem made you feel then, or makes you feel now. Nope! None of that, please.

One of the things we appreciate most about this system is that it helps us stay away from that sticky emotionally laden heavy stuff and have more fun! Yes, the system does ask us to reflect upon our life, and do positive, not negative recalling.

Because you will be doing positive recalling, and not looking back through the negative lens of fault-finding and problem analyzing, the exercises won't feel at all onerous. Quite the opposite. You will begin to feel a bit lighter and brighter each time you use one of them.

The lines of inquiry will help you find those things that you have already accomplished, things that did work and were useful, helpful, and meaningful. It is in those past good actions and choices that the clues to your future successes await to be rediscovered.

No matter what you say, we doubt that everything has gone wrong for you. We know there are things you know how to do, and at times in your life, you have employed one or more brilliant strokes of genius! You can always do so again. Why not?

We will guide you through a simple process of finding the clues to your success that can be modified to work for you in the present, so that you can construct doable solutions to work in your life right now.

Change Our Conversations, Change Our World

When we look back over our lives, the events that resist decay and stand out in our memories as significant are the ones that are meaningful to us. Most of these life-changing events involved the kind of unexpected shifts in the "tectonic plates" of our subconscious web of beliefs, such that their reverberations broke through into our consciousness.

What we mean by those semi-Freudian terms is simple. The events that we keep in our memories tend to be the ones that made us pause and consider who we really are in context of others in our lives.

These are life-changing moments when we encounter people or experiences that gave us a new perspective or vantage point about ourselves in a defining way. Though perhaps disorienting or unsettling, these shifts of our inner world are significant and meaningful to us as we make our way through life.

Looking at how or why these moments happened is interesting, but that they happened is of more relevance to where we go from here. Those significant moments, sometimes a simple pleasure, sometimes something born of a great challenge, give us the resources we need when contemplating next steps in our lives.

These moments can yet again become a catalyst—as they were, after all, you being "the right person, at the right time, saying or doing the right thing."

Perhaps a mentor, a spiritual guide or friend helped you make those seismic shifts, the needed changes and adjustments that got you through the changes. But, you had to decide to use their support. One thing we know for sure: Your conversation, the words you used, your perspective before and after those life-changing events were altered by those shifts.

We hope, whether we nudge you to changes high or low on the Richter scale, (and you'll decide how big or small you want those shifts to be), to once again alter some significant words and perspectives, and thus conversations, in your life.

Life-changing conversations then, are the ones that are transactional, exchanging or adding some new information, perhaps even skills or interpersonal muscle that we haven't flexed before. They involve engagement that results in the slight yet noticeable re-arrangement of our basic assumptions. When we actively seek significant change in our lives, we inevitably pursue conversations (with ourselves and others) that change how we think, how we feel, and also, inevitably, how we act.

If there is anything this book is about, it is about the doing of something new, however slightly new that doing may be. It may mean that we first have to change how we think or feel about something.

Some techniques in this book will seem so simple that you might underestimate how powerfully they could change your world.

Solutions are not significant if they sit in the brain or pool around the heart. They're maybe interesting insights and when conveyed in a motivational speech, provocative of strong feelings. But, in the end, if that's all that happens, we, the co-authors of this book, have to ask, "So what?"

Changing our conversations needs be a doing thing, not only a thinking, feeling thing, although thoughts and feelings are inevitable by-products. All that we're saying here is that when you change your conversation, you really do change your world, but only when those conversations move out of your head and heart into doable actions that give others the chance to experience you in new and different ways.

What you say (to yourself and others) can be powerful, but even more powerful is what you do (for yourself and others). Some techniques in this book will seem so simple that you might underestimate how powerfully they could change your world.

You would not be the first. We encountered these ideas, applied them and thought, "Well, it couldn't hurt." And we were right. It didn't hurt. But, we were also wrong. We also thought that maybe we would make a few little changes that would at least help us tolerate our circumstances.

We were way off. The few little changes kept adding up to bigger and bigger changes until our whole lives were changed, and yet, we were remarkably still ourselves!

What follows is a brief background that explains how, from very different professional and personal angles, the co-authors nonetheless developed a similar passion for changing conversations, and thus, changing their own and others' lives to the better.

Karen

Since 1997, I have been involved in United Nations liaison work, and for seven of those years I daily walked the corridors of its Headquarters in New York

Without going into a lot of detail, my work was to introduce the diplomatic community to innovative and sometimes politically challenging, international projects. I had a small staff, usually a few interns at a time that I would train, though there were as many as 85 at one point.

Essentially, my role was to initiate, motivate and organize small working groups of diplomats and their assistants to generate ideas toward needed projects, seminars, and conferences with United Nations goals in mind. One such effort brought together 500 women in the Middle East to consider inter-religious dialogue as one means of improving relationships between contentious entities in the area. It was then, and still is, a delicate work in progress.

On the strength of its international programs such as a woman's school for tribal reconciliation in Rwanda, I was privileged to help one NGO (non-governmental organization of the UN) obtain its goal to obtain special status in a core UN council, the ECOSOC (Economic and Social Council). This committee is a key decision-making body of the UN and only a very small percentage of the thousands of active NGOs are able to acquire membership and access to its inner workings.

I am still involved with international capacity building and education, along with NGO advocacy, albeit from the west coast. Throughout the years, I have had to distill into a few terse phrases, my endeavors at the UN. In doing so, I became keenly aware of how important brief encounters and exchanges are. Often, that was all I had with which to catch an ambassador's attention, spark their curiosity or help them see I represented something relevant to their concerns.

My interest in social change, and later realizations that the essence of any change began with new conversations, stemmed from my college studies. I majored in Physics, and still love the discipline. In my final year I added History and Philosophy of Science to my degree program.

I was fascinated as to how ideas arose, took hold and then later dissipated, often wrested violently within conflicted human dialogue as they emerged and competed for preeminence. Fortunately for me, the University of Melbourne was one of a very few universities in the world at that time that had a department and degree program in this particular area of study.

Thomas Kuhn, author of "Structure of Scientific Revolutions" had a profound impact on me. His ideas came back to me during my intensive years at the UN because it was at that time that the UN community was in the throes of an ongoing discussion about its "renewal." It was exciting for all of us involved, and the changes of conversation that occurred did indeed help the UN set a new course for itself in this century.

The fascinating thing about enormous change is that often people become impatient, don't want to take the many, many small steps that lead to real change, and instead opt for "short-cuts." What I mean by that is simple. They opt for war.

Renewal requires not just new projects, or resolutions, or a simple re-arrangement of the books on the coffee table. I came to see my work, in essence, to generate new conversations, via small working groups, larger committees and at times in large conferences such as the one described above. I knew that to change any conversation, we had to not only introduce new facts and figures, but we had to allow people to "see" differently, to envision differently and so to decide and act differently.

The fascinating thing about enormous change is that often people become impatient, don't want to take the many, many small steps that lead to real change, and instead opt for "short-cuts." What I mean by that is simple. They opt for war.

Likewise, on the micro level, we also opt for argument, raising our voice, imposing our will or cutting off the discussion altogether and stomping out of the room.

Being a working member of the UN, I prefer to assume there are alternatives to war, albeit historically they have not been practiced often enough, and remain elusive goals even today. Nonetheless, I have seen people transform and not only in response to violence and physical trauma. I have personally watched high level diplomats as well as grass roots volunteers engage in new conversations that have changed their world views.

I have seen people who held lifelong suspicions about one another come to realizations that they are not so different. These turnarounds do happen and when they can be sustained over time, there is dramatic change.

When I encountered the materials we present in this book, I had an "Aha" moment as I recognized a practical logic about change itself that could be applied at both the micro and macro levels. My choice for application was simple, however. I chose to start at the micro level, which meant myself and then others around me.

It is my hope that in time these same techniques can be employed at the macro level, a la Thomas Kuhn's concept of a paradigm shift, when "the right person presents the right idea in the right place at the right time."

I don't know who that right person will be, or when that right time will arrive, because I also fully recognize that humans change through a strange mix of the ordinary and the extraordinary. Regardless, your take away from all this is very simple: Changing your conversation is the beginning of what can be a profoundly life-changing experience.

I am sure you have already had such "conversations." Perhaps yours was an encounter that included little to few words, but the interaction nevertheless resulted in a significant change of how you now see and speak about certain things in your life.

If we see that our conversations are essentially our life experiences, our internal conversations, (our self-talk), our informal conversations with friends and family, along with our more formal discussions, debates and deliberations, we then have to ask, "If I intentionally change my conversations, will my whole life change?

And my answer is, "Yes!"

The two are so intertwined are they not? If you think about what it means to be alive, you begin to realize that the quality of life for those who cannot converse is very minimal.

The story of Helen Keller is compelling because it is a profound example of how conversation, simply the ability to converse at all, was enormously life changing for her. She not only escaped from a world of dark confusion, she went on to enlighten a nation as to how it could change its conversation toward those who have impairments of any kind.

So now, you can perhaps grasp how changing the conversations in your life will indeed change all aspects of your life, and that this is a pretty good thing. This book intends to help you do just that, create new ongoing conversations in your head and heart, and hopefully lighten up those darker corners, and make your world a brighter, better place.

Marilyn

My colleague and I are threading a bit of a fine line between education and entertainment in this book. However, if you don't mind a gentle poke in the ribs now and then, you'll be all right. We are both confident that you will be able to figure out when we're being serious and when we've got our tongues stuck to the inside of our cheeks.

What we have both wondered, for nearly all our adult lives, albeit from different vantage points of observing the human condition, is how do we change those vital conversations that leave lasting impact upon our lives? Not all conversations are serious, and we celebrate the times we engage with family and friends that fill us with laughter and leave us with good memories.

It is the other times, when conversation breaks down and we are left burdened with dark thoughts and intense, unwanted feelings that we hope to address here. Before I began to study the materials presented in this book, several of my vital conversations had deteriorated into trench wars, within myself and in relationship to others.

I was not only aware of how stuck I was in failing conversations, but also, as a person dispensing compassionate listening, pastoral counsel for loss and grief to patients and families in crises, I could clearly see others caught in similar dilemmas. This pained me even more.

As a professional hospital and hospice chaplain, I've been involved with a few thousand death and dying scenarios. I've held stillborn babies as small as my hand, and blessed them as their tearful parents held each other and wordlessly looked on. At the opposite end of life, I've chuckled along with a 106-year-old woman who asked me in exasperation, "For crying out loud, Chaplain, why am I still here?!"

Before I began to study the materials presented in this book, several of my vital conversations had deteriorated into trench wars, within myself and in relationship to others.

When I replied, "I don't know. Have you always had trouble making up your mind?" She looked at me, shocked at first, then laughed and replied, "No!" And then she remarked more thoughtfully as she looked out the window, "It's starting to snow. Today is as good a day as any other." She died within a few hours.

As part of a team of chaplains that served a large hospital system, I tended several emergency departments over nearly a decade and half. In that time, I prayed over victims of the worst kinds of violence and assisted families suffering through an endless array of tragedies, some so egregiously unfair they rendered me wondering what kind of God was running this universe, or if any "god" was out there at all.

These situations were hard to navigate, but the hardest for me was watching a loved one stand at bedside, looking down at their family member or close friend, and unable to say the words that were so obviously on their heart. My own heart would ache for them as they worked their jaw, but could not find a way to utter the words that would have meant so much for them to say and for the other to hear.

I fully understand that sometimes words cannot adequately convey what is deeply embedded in our emotions. I often give permission to those struggling in such situations to speak in the tongue we all have access to when words fails us–the language of tears.

In fact, I often give those struggling with their emotions permission to speak in the tongue we all have access to when words fails us, the language of tears.

I once experienced this with a man grieving the death of his mother. He was about twice my size and heavily tattooed, but in spite of his tough exterior, clearly needed to express his anguished feelings. I said, "If you need to cry, go ahead. I won't think the less of you." He turned away from me, his face so red I thought I must have angered him, but then to my surprise, he wheeled around, buried his head in my shoulder and wept.

Human conversations are complex, entangled, often difficult and at odds with the intentions of those involved in them. We need not be morose, however. Our conversations are also happy and fun. They light up our lives and we treasure them. As I've said, the happy conversations are not the ones we need to change.

The ones we need to change are the ruts of negative self-talk and the conflicted conversations with others that seem to never resolve. These are conversations we so very much long to change, and yet we wonder, how?

How do we lighten up on ourselves? How do we change that inner conversation of self-recrimination, where we name, shame and blame ourselves over mistakes that we allow others to make, but not ourselves?

How do we change the conversations with those we want to love, but with whom things have fallen into such disrepair that all that is left is an age old tired argument that feels like "deja vu, all over again?" How do we change the conversation with our children, young or adult, or with friends, colleagues, and bosses?

Where do we start? How do we take a different path that leads us to define who we really are, so that we can tell others more clearly about our real thoughts and feelings?

How do we define what we really want, not selfishly, but in regard to others, and still, what we really want? How do we avoid falling into wordlessness when we come to those all important moments, be they when someone we love is dying, or simply when someone we love is sitting across the table from us with a quizzical look on their face? I wanted to know this, with all my heart, for much of my life.

Since I was very young I've been a writer, and have written an array of short stories, poems and songs. In college, I received commendation for my academic papers. In short, I am an articulate person–on paper. However, in conversation, I am often quite the opposite, at times incapable of clearly explaining myself when it counted most. I was one of those persons at bedside, working my jaw, but caught in a complex of emotions that would not lend themselves to verbal expression.

I wanted to change, and for the few who wanted me to stay in my unhappy, unhealthy, non-functional conversant state, all I can say is, call me when you're ready to engage the real me that I've finally allowed myself to become.

I so wanted to change the difficult conversations in my life, but how?!

In mid-life, I struggled to communicate with close family members about things in my heart that needed healing. At work, I found myself silent in the face of a boss who misunderstood nearly everything about me, and preferred me to subdue my forthright character so he would not have to deal with me. It was stifling.

At that time in my life, I was the mother of teenagers, a houseful of them, between 13 and 19 years of age. Talk about conversations that needed changing! All I wanted was to communicate without one of us flaring into an angry outburst. Don't get me wrong. I often laughed with my family as we had our share of good times together, but when you have a houseful of teenagers, conversations seem to break down on a daily basis.

What I've learned since those times is how to have healthier, happier conversations. The essence of that learning is contained in this book. Though again, learning the techniques is not an end all and be all.

I had to apply them in relationship to others. Not everyone reacted the same: Some allowed me to become a better version of myself, and others wanted the silent, perplexed philosopher to remain her sullen self, because that's the person they were familiar with.

I wanted to change, and for the few who wanted me to stay in my unhappy, unhealthy, non-functional conversant state, all I can say is, call me when you're ready to engage the real me that I've finally allowed myself to become.

My now adult children hear me speak in clear language about who I am and what I want. And, equally, perhaps even more importantly, I listen for the same from them. We are able to be much more honest without pointing fingers and making accusations.

We say those important words, too. The last thing I want to do with those words is wait. I have happier and healthier conversations at work with my colleagues and bosses. I'm able to be my creative self and fit into the corporate world, for the most part. Learning how to have such conversations has changed not only my self and other talk, it has, quite frankly, changed my life, how I wake up, get through the day, and go to sleep.

Am I now completely cured? *No!* I still have times when I'm anxious and cannot say what I want in that moment. However, no longer do I wallow in the muck of self-doubt and double-checking, and now more freely speak my mind and share my heart when I'm ready to do so.

What I've learned, what my co-author and I will try to share with you in the pages that follow, are several little things, that when compiled together can change how you think, feel, work, and interact with the important other people in your life.

One thing that took me a long time to believe, and thus practice, is that I'm the expert of my life. Trusting myself as the expert of myself, was, and remains, a most profound mind and heart-changing journey.

Several years ago, I had the good fortune of working with an excellent therapist who was the right person at the right time in my life. Even so, I could not rely on her to figure me out. She often had to remind me that the only person who could figure me out was, well, me!

We hope what you learn in the pages that follow not only give you some serious food for thought, but also make you smile, and bring you moments of "Aha!" and self-recognition.

Changing the conversation in my head was not easy. In fact, it was so difficult that I had to start with changing how I conversed with others, and then work inward from there. You might choose to go at things in the opposite direction. That will be perfectly fine, and you'll learn why that's so in subsequent chapters.

What we, Karen and I, want to leave you with is this: If you are struggling to change the conversations in your life, you are very much not alone. We both have watched our fellow human beings struggle to have meaningful, constructive conversations, at the micro and macro levels of their endeavoring, and in so doing, we noticed the same struggle in ourselves.

This book is yet another beginning of our own changing of conversations, as one thing we've learned, we are always at the beginning, again and again. We hope what you learn in the pages that follow not only give you some serious food for thought, but also make you smile, and bring you moments of "Aha!" and self recognition. We further hope that many times you will think, "Well, that's so simple, why didn't I already think of it?"

If that's often your conclusion, and because it does seem so simple, you actually try out the techniques to some degree of success, then we will have accomplished our mission. That is, to give others the same chance we offered ourselves—a way to change the conversations that meant most to us.

In all seriousness, we simply hope you find this book useful, and in all non-seriousness, we hope you have fun with it, too. The essential part of fun is surprise. When we become open to letting the unexpected happen, guess what? It happens!

It really is true that we can never quite know what the future holds. Gaining confidence in being my real self and discovering that the unexpected was something I could handle has given me a most "unexpected" gift. It has re-infused my life with the joy of living as a creative being, letting myself, and others, be free to explore and experience who we truly are in relationship with one another.

Here's to yet another beginning for you, in the journey toward the rest of your unexpected life. Here's to learning how to discover yourself in new thoughts, feelings, and what may have been unexpressed hopes. Most of all, here's to your new, happier, healthier conversations. In short, here's to you becoming someone you've always wanted to be ... your very own real self.

Part II: BREAKING THE CHAINS

2. The 3 BIG Mistakes We All Make!

Yeah, Problems Are Hard. Or Are They?

Do you remember the elementary book titled, "Stop that Ball?" In a clever way, the author wanted to introduce young readers to various roles of adults in a local town, a grocer, barber, police officer, postman, baker, etc. The story is simple. A boy is bouncing a beach ball in his backyard. He bounced it a bit too high, the wind picked it up over the fence and away it went, giving the boy an opportunity to chase it through the town, shouting, "Stop that ball!"

Eventually, boy and beach ball are reunited. He returns to happily bouncing it in his backyard when … yep, he forgets, bounces the ball a bit too high, and once again, the wind picks it up and over the fence it goes. The story ends with the boy shouting as he runs out the gate, "Stop that ball!"

When we think about the problems in our lives, isn't this a near perfect analogy as to how they seem to never quite go away? We go all around our "town," telling everyone our problem, sometimes asking for their help or advice, and just when we think we have the situation resolved, up over the fence the darn thing flies and we have to chase it all over again.

We're here to tell you something very startling. And we'll explain exactly why we're confident to say this. In this section, you are going to learn how to break the chains from your problems. Of course, you will still have to work on solutions, which we help you to understand in the next section, "Set Your Course." And happily, as you work your way through that section, you will discover that within yourself and in relation to others, you are changing the conversations in your life, innovating and invigorating your life as you've never before imagined, or at least, not for quite some time.

The biggest mistake we all make when it comes to solving personal problems is that we think we have to know as much as we possibly can about the problem in order to solve it.

But here, in this first section, you are going to discover that when your problem once again escapes from the fence that you've set around it, you won't have to run around like a perplexed chicken with the proverbial severed head trying to get that thing to stop. Never again will you have to feel defeated by a problem, unless you really want to have problems wrapped around your body like a hundred pound chain attached to a concrete block that weighs you down to the bottom of a river.

Before we start with the "what to do's" for solving your problems, we want to clear the path in front of you from some essential "what NOT to do's." Don't worry. There are only three (just 3) big mistakes that we hope to prevent you from making.

These are mistakes we all make, and almost all the time, so no need to feel bad as you read along. And sure, the list of awful mistakes we commonly make when dealing with problems is much longer, but these are the 3 that will impede your progress the most. If you avoid these, you will progress quickly. That's why we focus on them up front. And since this is self-help, you need to be aware of them so you can catch yourself!

Big Mistake #1
The biggest one we all have made and a total solution kill

Now, let's say you are a normal western educated human being. If so, you will find the #1 big mistake difficult to believe at first. That's because it is counter to just about the entire intellectual sweep of Euro-American culture. So, the first time it's presented, your mind may come to something of a stop, or what many of Karen's students have described as a "brain freeze."

Here's why. The biggest mistake we all make when it comes to solving personal problems is that we think we have to know as much as we possibly can about the problem in order to solve it. Such expert knowledge is usually constructed around "why." We intend you show you from a number of perspectives that this assumption is flat out wrong.

Our western civilization is largely based upon the scientific method of inquiry. Without it we would not be where we are today. It is a marvelous invention of the mind, and when it comes to mechanical, technical problems, its effectiveness is absolutely unparalleled. There is a "caveat" here, and not about the scientific method, but in how many people have adopted some misconceptions about it.

Good problem solving is all about new thinking and innovative actions stimulated by a problem. This is the very important distinction between being a solution creator/builder /constructor and a Problem Expert.

The biggest mistake comes when people think that the scientific method deems "a problem can't be solved if it isn't understood." In many cases, this is a simple explanation given along with the first step in the scientific process in schools.

The myth for many of us, regarding the scientific method, is that we *can* understand the "why" of the problem and it is that understanding which allows us to solve it. But in truth, the scientific method urges us toward something different: the exploration of one (or many), possible solutions to the problem that has come to our attention.

Further it encourages us to engage in an iterative process starting with some basic elements we choose precisely because we know they have worked in the past. Problem solving as we're proposing is consistent with the scientific method and is really all about creating solutions.

Good problem solving is all about new thinking and innovative actions *stimulated by* a problem. This is the very important distinction between being a solution creator/builder/constructor and a Problem Expert.

Problems are not solved by clinging to the history of how and why the problem emerged, digging ever deeper and wider, even if we do end up with better descriptions of the problems in 3-D Technicolor.

The activity of creating solutions is vastly different than that of asking why or analyzing a problem for the purpose of assigning blame or for seeking approval or absolution or justice. Analysis from each of those perspectives can have their own outcomes, but none of those activities actually create vital solutions for our lives.

What we can confidently say is that whatever the thinking that resulted in the problem, the assumptions, beliefs, and practices are what secured the problem in the first place. Holding onto prior assumptions, beliefs and practices is what *not* to do if we don't want the problem to persist. Finding something different to do gives us a much better chance of getting a better result.

In short, our understanding of "problem solving" gets confused when we don't get past the very first step of the creative scientific process where we "state the problem." Like a moth to a flame, we are so entangled with the emotional aspects of the problem that we spend all our time becoming Problem Experts, and we don't take that next crucial step of developing a novel hypothesis to test, something new to try for this particular situation, a change in conversation and action, to get us moving forward.

To stay in the pain of the problem is not only unhelpful, it is enormously time and energy consuming. Look around you. How many people do you know seem to love their misery even though it is exhausting to continually re-experience their thoughts and feelings as they delve deeper and deeper into why their problem exists, how it all began, who's to blame, and so forth.

This kind of problem focusing turns us into only one thing: a "Problem Expert." And there's an enormous cost to being one. Consider this. 77% Americans suffer from one or several physical symptoms of stress. What if they were busy instead having fun while solving their problems rather than wallowing in misery and not resolving them?

Think about the stress that one simple problem causes you when you stew over it. Add up all the problems you encounter in one day, be it dealing with commuter traffic, listening to an annoying co-worker, handling difficult customers, working with reluctant subordinates, figuring out what your boss wants, trying to reason with your teenager, and so forth.

Problem Experts stew and stew, but all this does is eventually deplete them of the energy needed to solve their problems. Talk about a conundrum!

To help you really get a clear picture of how costly it is, merely in terms of time spent, think about this. If you spend only 30 minutes a day, 5-10 minutes here and there, worrying, ruminating and re-living this or that problem, those 30 minutes a day translate into 4.56 forty-hour work weeks a year!!!

Yes, we're talking about those times you tell the story again about your bad boss, your impossible neighbor, or difficult child to yet another person.

So basically add up the time you spend rolling your eyes, gritting your teeth, lying awake at night, seething with anger and replaying those difficult conversations you can't believe really happened. You're spending one working month out of every year worrying and very likely not solving anything. It's as if all you did for that month was re-hash the problem, all day long!

If you spend an hour a day like that, then you've wasted two whole months of work on the problem, precious time you could have (and will, by the time you finish this book) spend more productively and happily!

Now, couple that with something quite interesting from a national survey. When asked on a LinkedIn survey that was posted in 2014, "what one thing do you long to have more of in your life, in one word?" the vast majority of people consider the #1 thing they wanted more of in their life is … *TIME*.

We're just given you a real number crunch as to how you're probably spending a great deal of time unnecessarily as a Problem Expert, mulling over all the where, when, why and how of your problems. The cost of not learning how to quickly move beyond problems is really very high, cutting into the one thing we value most.

And it gets worse. Worry causes stress. Stress causes all kinds of unhealthy havoc on the body. The articles and books about that are endless. Suffice to say, we can attribute many of our modern illnesses to stress and the behaviors that it causes (overeating, drinking to excess, smoking, getting angry at oneself and others, etc.).

What if we could offer you another way to go about your life that did not include constantly worrying and emotionally re-living problems, instead resolving them and moving forward in an authentic, meaningful and joyful way, all with a big, huge bonus? And that is, a clear mind and peaceful heart. Would you take us up on it? We hope so.

If you are ready for that first step toward a problems-less/solutions-more lifestyle, we are ready to give you what Karen calls, "The Big Idea."

So, here's the #1 thing you need to realize from here on in:

You do not need to know anything about your problem in order to create an effective solution for it.

If you are thinking, "What?! Are they for real?" we suggest you read that sentence again, slowly and softly to yourself, inserting "I" for "you." Oh, forget the whisper. Just say it out aloud.

"I do not need to know anything about my problem in order to create an effective solution for it."

Notice the resistance in your brain. You might be hearing something like, "Huh? No way that's true! Of course I have to know everything about my issues if I'm ever going to fix them. What do you mean?!"

Well, we mean exactly what we wrote. Now, the rare person might think otherwise and agree with us from the get-go, but to be honest, we have yet to meet him or her. So then, need we repeat the above? Yes, and we will.

We know this because even after years of practicing this system, we still have to remind ourselves not to dwell on or be seduced by the problem facing us. Bottom line is that we are, and you are, so very humanly prone to continually repeat this #1 biggest mistake.

Sure, it's good to know you have a problem. If you're blind to the fact that something is wrong, then of course, you won't have any motivation to change it. Other than that, once you learn the techniques in this book, you will no longer need to continually worry about, mull over, lose sleep because of, or "rake the muck" of your problem over and over again (ad nauseam). In our words, you don't have to remain an overburdened Problem Expert.

We give you a tool that you can reach for when the "and gloom loop" or the more subtle under-miner of vitality—procrastination—tries to trip you up. And we give you another tool for when you are frozen in a state of pre-explosive frustration, when you are desperate to change your circumstance, but just don't know what *to* do.

How many times have you been immobilized yet desperate for change at the same time, frozen like a deer in the headlights because you just don't know what to do? How often do you find yourself in a state where your brain is flooded with stress-inducing neuro-transmitters? And, how do feel when you search your mind and heart for how to alleviate what you perceive as a moral dilemma, and find no answers?

We take you outside these seemingly hopeless situations by allowing you to not buy into the ruse of the problem—that you have to defeat it! You don't have to defeat the problem. You don't even have to pay attention to it (unless you want to), because you don't have to keep playing the same mind-games that created the problem in the first place.

"The world as we have created it is a process of our thinking. It cannot be changed without changing our thinking."

"A clever person solves a problem. A wise person avoids it."

"If we knew what it was we were doing, it would not be called research, would it?"

— Albert Einstein

Now, to visually show the extreme complications of being a Problem Expert we put this graphic together where "You" are in the square depicting all that a Problem Expert has to contend with. Hey, it's not just you. We're in that same box with you.

Most problems rarely stand alone in our lives. They interweave throughout our relationships, doubling and tripling their effect upon us. Doesn't that "You" box look and feel crowded in?

On top of the simple complexity of our lives, when we then analyze each aspect of each of the influences on each problem, forever in search of the magical thread that will unravel it all with one magical tug, we are steeping ourselves in the accompanying emotional toxicity more and more. This is unhealthy and we are using precious time and energy on the rather futile microscopic inspection of what we know doesn't work rather than investing that same time and energy in actions that will bring us new outcomes.

At some point in our lives many of us falter under the weight of our rather amazing but complex lives. We become immobilized. We simply give up, hunker down, plow ahead and live our lives with the least amount of misery we can bear. This all adds up to one huge impact upon our innately happiness-seeking selves. (You do want to be happy, don't you?). In a word: We *stress*.

Stress leads to a multitude of mental and physical "diseases" that have created a multi-billion dollar complex industry to deal with its fallout. We take all manner of medicines and herbs to counter the head and body aches caused by stress.

Sometimes the medicines have side effects that cause us further stress. Also, we often unknowingly self-medicate, i.e., drink a bit too much, party a little too hardy, watch too much TV and ignore the people we live with day to day, gamble more than we can afford, and engage in other unhealthy habits.

What if there was a way to alleviate the stress of being a Problem Expert? What if there was a way to discontinue our daily focusing on problems? What if we didn't have the weight of those problems crushing down upon us from the moment we wake until we go to sleep (only to wake again in the wee hours to one more time scour our brain for something we might have missed about those problems)?

Happily, there is a way, and we're going to show you, step by simple step. We're also going to give you several shortcut methods that will shift you from being a Problem Expert to becoming a Solutions Master. But first, (sorry for the delay), we have to forewarn you about two other (only 2 more) big mistakes that make forward progress difficult.

Big Mistake #2
Not quite as big as #1,
but just as much of a solution kill

Most people think, quite naturally, that if a problem is a complicated, they need a complicated solution to fix it. Again, we have a counter-intuitive, counter-culture (as our current techno-centric culture is oriented to complexity) to offer you. Here it is:

The simpler the steps in a solution, the more likely we are to use them and thus to succeed.

Solutions do not have to be complicated in order to solve difficult problems.

It's embarrassing at first to think that small, doable steps could indeed solve those gnarly problems that bedevil us. I mean, don't your problems sometimes seem to lurch around in your life like a B-grade invading alien movie monster? We somehow can't find a way to resolve them, no matter how much we desperately want to. Sadly then, we come to the conclusion that without some kind of intricately designed, high-tech death ray type of whirly-gig tool, we'll never get rid of them.

However, pause to consider how those problems gathered around you. They usually started out rather innocuously and grew, bit by bit, over time. In the same way then, you can apply solutions, starting out with seemingly small changes that will eventually accumulate and lead to bigger changes. We'll speak more to this a bit later.

A few of you might be thinking, "That's not so counter-culture, is it? To which we reply that if you are not sure we live in a complicated world, then you probably haven't been following the news or paid your taxes in a while.

Once you make the shift from believing you must focus on your problems in order to solve them, you can begin to spend your precious time and energy envisioning solutions and creating the steps needed to implement them.

Again, don't worry just yet how to do the things we're introducing here. We will show you how to make the shift away from Big Mistakes #1 and #2 and likewise, we'll show you how to develop and implement the doable steps to solve your problem(s). And, and, and, a whole bunch more of other neat short cuts. Bear with us. There is a method to our method.

Big Mistake #3
A subtle, but also effective solution killer

Let's just get this one onto the table right away:

> *You don't need an intense "fire in the belly" motivation to achieve the solutions you create for your problem.*

Seriously. How much motivation is enough motivation? Of course, if you cannot get out of bed due to feeling overwhelmed by your problems, then maybe you should refer to our disclaimer in the introduction and seek the professional help you need to get out of bed.

As soon as you are able to do that, and maybe make some toast with a cup of tea or coffee, get back to us. Because at that point, you can probably do a good bit of, if not yet all the steps provided in this book. They are that easy to understand and, if you want to do them, they are that easy to do.

Remember what we said in the introduction about will power and persistence? Science shows that these and other conscious efforts toward change are only 2%-4% of our thought patterns and behavior involved? We don't focus on will power and perseverance because it isn't an effective strategy.

We focus instead on finding ways to do something, anything, different from whatever we were doing that got us into the problem in the first place.

We've researched a lot of self-help programs. Almost all of them require their adherents to maintain rather high levels of motivation to begin, get through and finish their proposed agenda. Don't get us wrong. We also think motivation is helpful. A person's steady commitment to a goal is a big boost. But does it need to be Herculean? We don't think you need more than a normal amount of desire to change to get you started on a path where you enjoy your advances that you soon *want* to keep using your new-found, vital-living system.

Think of when you purchased your first smart phone. It didn't take you long to get past "how do I use this darn thing?" to where you wouldn't leave your house without it.

And if you do leave your house without it, you soon turn around to go back and get it. Are we right? Further, for 80% of us, it's the first thing we reach for in the morning before we head to the bathroom. Talk about a change in daily habits!

Our point is simple. If you have enough motivation to get out of bed in the morning, you've probably got enough to start and follow through with this program. Once out of bed, you can slip and slide all over the map through your problems and the solutions you envision for them. That would be so human of you.

Yep, about 15 seconds is all it takes to make the first shift from the Problem Expert to a Solutions Master mode.

After all, if we aren't encountering setbacks, we probably aren't trying to do something different. If there's one thing this program will encourage you to do, it will be something, anything different from what you've already been doing.

And here's a bonus! We've got the slip and slide phenomena covered because we'll also show you how to handle setbacks in a useful way. In fact, setbacks won't even be setbacks. (Ha, ha, but we do mean it). They'll be points of insight, and at the least, stumbles forward. But, if you follow only this one of the five main techniques in this system, setbacks will become your favorite source of information, and even motivate you to keep moving forward.

You don't need to think too long and hard about any aspect of the Solutions System either. The Matrix quickly becomes a way to think about, and begin to love again, your life. Yes, even the parts of it you have long been convinced were unlovable.

So you don't need to go off to an expensive seminar in a New Mexico desert or sit atop an Asian mountain in order to gather your thoughts and align your emotions. None of that is needed, though if you want to attend these things, we'll certainly not stop you.

We are not against seminars and retreats. We've been there, done all that, and have the charges on our old credit cards to prove it. While seminars and retreats can be helpful, you don't *have* to do any of that in our program to get amazing results.

What we've discovered is that each little thing we do, even in the first few seconds when a problem confronts us, makes all the difference in the world.

Yep, about 15 seconds is all it takes to make the first shift from the Problem Expert to a Solutions Master mode. Our brains can think really, really fast. It's astonishing just how much we process, in a positive or negative direction, in the few blinks of a 15-second interval.

Consider this little factoid: We read at a rate of about 200-300 words per minute (wpm). We listen to books on tape at the rate of about 150-160 wpm. We are able to comprehend most of what auctioneers say at a rate of around 300-400 wpm. But, when we think, whew, we are like greased lightning! Okay, few things in the universe are as fast as lightning, but we think at an amazing speed, estimated at 1300 wpm.

Why bring up all this brain stuff? Because, when problems confront us, as they do all the time, we can quickly think through an effective step toward a solution. If you take those 15 seconds, multiply them by 1300 words per minute; you come up with about 2 minutes of a book on tape. (1300/4 = 325 words).

What does that mean for you? It means that it doesn't take all that much to think of a single, small, simple step to respond to a big hunk of a problem. You can chip away at those problems as they arise. You won't solve everything all at once. We don't promise anything like that. But, you will be able to do *something*, not *nothing*, about your problems, each and every day. That's big. That's huge!

Just think what this will do for your health if you are able to turn yourself away from immersing in high stress habits, and instead spend your time on oxytocin (natural happiness chemicals in your brain) inducing behavior. We will show you just how small changes accumulate into larger changes, the way money compounds in a bank account, what Albert Einstein deemed as one of the greatest inventions of the modern era.

Karen

By the way, here's the math on compounding. Would you rather have a million dollars up front, or set aside a penny and have it doubled each day for a month? If you suspected the penny a day doubled for a month could end up more than a million dollars, you are right.

It adds up to one million dollars vs. $2,684,354.56 after 30 days and by 31 days it's $5,368,709.12! So *do not* under estimate the power of the small. Life doesn't happen in a straight line. And when you deal with biology, it tends to be exponential. The compounding effects of small positive changes are also huge—just as are the effects of negative changes. So give yourself a chance and make great, small changes!

Remember, these small changes are further magnified by environment, moods, politics, religion, hormones, how people respond to our changes, and even the weather itself. We're simply encouraging you not to be daunted by yet another self-help promise that seems too big to be true. We aren't making big promises, but we are promising that small changes add up to big effects.

We understand that problems hurt. We've been there in many a dark night wrestling with our souls. We've suffered health problems, job problems, spouse problems, financial problems, teenager problems (multiple times with those and yet, they've all become pretty decent adults), along with bad bosses, conniving colleagues, and a few friends that turned out to be less than fair weather companions to say nothing of organizations that gladly took years of our lives, and though we accomplished much, nonetheless, kicked us to the curb without a second thought when it suited their financial interest.

The point is, we made significant changes over time, and you can do so as well. Don't worry if you don't happen to have the deepest gut-level desire to solve all your problems. That energy may well have already been sapped out of you. Just wanting to make one problem a little less of a pain than it currently is will be enough to start.

As you go along, and begin to discover how much fun these techniques can be, you'll feel better. When you feel better, you want to do even more. Soon, you'll be doubling those small changes each day. Remember the compounded pennies? You're going to become a Solutions Master millionaire in no time, well in some time, but not in the amount of time you might be thinking it will take.

Another Disclaimer:
What this program is and is *not*.

Results will vary. People are different. Don't worry about how fast or slow you seem to be progressing. We've heard it all from those who learn and practice this method. There are inevitable ups and downs. There are curve balls and odd things that we just didn't see coming. Hey, that's life!

What we don't provide in this book is blame or guilt or finger wagging, or any reason for you to think you aren't adequate or up to demands of the program. The system doesn't have demands, per se. In fact, it will alleviate some of the demands you feel that you or others have placed upon you, unless you want to have those demands, and if so, then don't disregard them.

The book was designed to be brief. If you want the same information in a heavily footnoted, laced with academic terminology format, check out our resource section. There are many of those resources, and we can show even more, but we'd have to send you a selfie photo in front of Karen's library shelves.

Not a Disclaimer:
Just helpful information
about the authors and this little book

In case you have an interest, here is a bit more information about the core components of the Solutions Mastery System and the co-authors of this book. While it is a little book, it does not come from a little bit of research, nor a little bit of life experience.

Karen has spent much of her adult career life dealing with complex group dynamics, whether it was teaching navigational skills to a room full of new boat captains, developing a domestic and international tour business, or negotiating the intricate protocols of the United Nations.

She designed and taught "Dramatic Change: Leveraging Personal Power to Impact Society Through Advocacy and Leadership" courses in the United States and abroad. Later, she encountered the academic and clinical research of Solution Focused Brief Therapy that now underlie the core aspects of her Solutions Mastery System (the System).

Because of her extensive experience in change leadership, she readily understood the importance of these materials and knew the impact they could make if properly rendered into a format for wider public consumption.

When Karen encountered these concepts, she recalled her first response being, "Whew, somebody's already formulated what's been stewing in my head and heart for years!" From there, she adapted the material into an online training course, distilled it into non-academic language, and finally honed it all into a self-help model that has been used by a wide range of participants.

This book, by the way, as we're still in the spirit of disclaiming, is not intended to be a full-on experience of the Solutions Mastery System. But it does provide essentials, and most importantly, an overview of the System with instructions how to use it. All the concepts we share with you ideas can be immediately applied.

The System is exquisitely simple: shift your focus from problems to solutions, adapt anew what has already worked for you, keep tabs on your progress and do more of what works best while at the same time discontinuing what doesn't work.

But as simple a self-help system as it is, for those of you that are encountering this kind of approach for the first time, we needed to "set the stage" for your success, and that meant a major mindset shift.

This shift from being a Problem Expert to becoming a Solutions Master is a bit like an earthquake in your ethos, your network of attitudes and habitual dispositions that predetermine your behaviors. This shake-up will continue to happen, but more easily now that you've had that first initial shock and your brain has begun to thaw.

The new framework we teach in this book frees you from having to know anything about whatever problem you have. That freedom provides a new opportunity for you to look at problems from an entirely different point of view.

The system outlined in the coming pages provides a structure, that when used on a regular basis, is nothing short of liberating. It's not about formulaic sayings or prayers, guided meditations or formal practices. It is totally customizable to your life. In fact, the only way it won't work for you is if you don't use it!

To repeat ourselves, the only way it doesn't work is if you don't use it!

It has taken years for us to get to this point, where we can share with you in an easy to read format how the Solutions Mastery System applies in daily practice. Like making a really good sauce in the kitchen, reducing something down to its essentials intensifies its potency.

The ideas presented in this book are derived from solid sources widely practiced in both clinical and non-clinical settings. But the academic literature about it is rather dense. Nonetheless, the concepts are amazingly adaptable for all kinds of practical use. We have extensively explored this material, used it on ourselves and taught it to others with an astonishing degree of success.

In the next chapter, we will continue with the underlying concepts that will help you lay the groundwork toward your solutions. We're excited for you. It won't be long before you're on your way from being an overburdened Problem Expert to standing tall as a proficient Solutions Master.

3. Principles at Play
No Matter What We Do

In this chapter, we are going to discuss the most essential principles at play that are always happening, whether we are aware of them or not.

Of course, there are a multitude of constants that hold this universe together, as well as principles that underlie our human existence, both individually and socially. Within Solution Focused Brief Therapy, there are more principles outlined than the ones we've chosen. The ones we give you in this chapter come from years of studying and practicing, and honing things down to their most useful essence for self-help.

First, a principle is reliable and always at work. You can be awake and aware, or asleep and unaware (or somewhere in between), and a principle will still be ongoing. You can resist and curse a principle, or accept and use it, and it won't care either way. It just is what it is.

It isn't that principles impose their will upon us. It's just that they do what they do whether we take interest in or ignore them. This is truly a cool thing, however, because when we align with these basic principles, and put them to use, it's as if we've added jet fuel to an engine.

Leveraging these principles makes us more efficient and effective. Simply put, everything goes a lot faster.

The Principles below are what we have found to be essential to keep in mind as you work through the Solutions Mastery System. You can find a one-page synopsis of these basic Principles, along with their accompanying Rules of Thumb, which we explain in the following chapter.

Principles of Change

1. Change is always happening

Karen

This is probably my favorite Principle. In fact for me it's not a matter of "if" change is happening, rather "how" change is happening. A more ancient version of that is, "No one steps into the same river twice." And then, there are discussions of how change happens in the universe at the subatomic levels, but I will spare you—today.

This principle is so innocuously at work that even though a major religion such as Buddhism makes it a primary tenet, we still often fail to recognize it. But we don't just fail to recognize the impermanence of everything. Society seems to implicitly dislike change. Why do we say that?

Take a look in the thesaurus at "homeostasis." Some beautiful words have evolved around "keeping things the same," even though as a reality, it is far from possible to do. Words like "equilibrium," "equanimity," "evenness," "stability," "equipoise," are all positive, even noble sounding words.

But, where are the equally aspirational words about "change?" Words such as "reversal," "adjustment," "mutation, "revolution" and "vicissitude" convey that change is less than desirable. A cursory lingual comparison reveals that we prefer "stasis," even though it's never actually possible in the human experience. All living things change, constantly.

Reactions such as "No! No! No!" when it comes to change are so natural to us that we don't notice how much we resist something just because it *might* change us. This odd human default has us fighting reality almost every step of the way.

Similar negative views about change are held across a wide spectrum of cultures. Let's reconsider Buddhism again for a moment, and we are looking at it here because more than any other cultural philosophy, the inevitability of change is a core tenet.

True, Buddhists are encouraged to embrace impermanence, but in the sense that not doing so causes suffering, and so, acceptance of change is something we humans simply must endure.

Refusing to accept that change is happening leads us down paths of discontent and unhappiness. Hospice chaplains see this in their line of work all the time. Of course, it is natural to resist death as a form of change because the enormity of that unknown elicits fear and the impending losses can be unimaginable.

...the issue is not whether you can make a difference, but what kind of difference you want to make.

So it's not your fault that you feel something in the pit of your stomach when you are about to make a change. We just hope you will begin to interpret that twist in your gut as excitement and anticipation, and not only as a girding for what might be some kind of loss. Instead, we hold out that the excitement of innovation, opportunity and renewal is what change can soon become for you!

In the end, no matter what we do, change is always happening in the universe, and in our lives. Acceptance of change can be misunderstood as fatalism. We want to strongly emphasize that the acceptance of change we refer to here is exactly the opposite of fatalism. When we accept that change *is always happening*, next we notice that one of two things occurs.

We can acknowledge that things just might get better. On the other hand, we can also (and probably usually assume) they might get worse. But for sure, nothing is going to stay the same. So, the very idea that no matter what, something *will* be different allows us to imagine life in any other way than our current experience.

We understand that it can be hard to accept that change really is happening, when you are hunkered down in the middle of a mess that feels enormous and immutable. Nonetheless, this principle is in effect, so somehow, some way, not only your life, but also something in your problem *will* change, even if you do nothing.

What is important to know is that we can lean into the force of this principle. We can use the knowledge that change is always happening to allow ourselves the opportunity to envision something other than the problem itself. It is simply a matter of being able to ask effective questions.

As to asking the right questions, Karen honed this part of the System down to 5 lines of inquiry (the Matrix). You can certainly devise other questions, but in the beginning, these lines of inquiry seem to get the whole wad of wax unstuck most effectively. Plus, the average person, as we are, seems to work best when given 3-5 steps. Otherwise, this book would start to feel like an instruction sheet for putting together furniture delivered in a box.

Take comfort in the fact that you are not bound to experience your problem in the same way one day to the next. If you're familiar with the movie "Groundhog Day," you'll recall how the lead character was trapped in reliving the same day, again and again, to the point where he devised several ways to end his life, only to wake up at the same time in the same place on what should have been another day, but somehow wasn't.

And yet, even here, change kept occurring in subtle ways, such that Phil, when attuned to that fact, eventually decided to live that same day, only differently each time he woke up in it. He started exploring what happened when he made different choices. Once he managed to do this, it no longer mattered that he was stuck in a bizarre time limbo on the 2nd day of February. He discovered it was his chance to experiment with doing things differently to see what resulted.

It was then that the problem of his circumstances was no longer a problem, rather a new opportunity in life that had emerged for him. Ultimately, when he was released into a whole new day, his situation was so profoundly different that instead of wanting nothing but to escape Punxsutawney, PA, he smiled and said, "Let's live here." This leads us directly to the next Principle of Change.

2. Small changes accumulate into bigger changes

Marilyn

As long as we're claiming favorite principles, I personally love this one. Learning to "appreciate the power of the small," of which Karen reminds me often, relieves me from wanting to save the world in my lifetime (don't ask for details, but yes, I tried).

When I was faced with some very serious problems (recall my "before" list), and felt as if I had nowhere to turn, no one to talk to and no way to change anything, I was in profound despair. Hopelessness is a debilitating emotion. It left me nearly paralyzed. I was not able to fathom how my life could ever be different. This was at a time when I was ascending the corporate ladder, so I also felt I had no right to complain about my life. In fact, a few persons I had sought for counsel had implied as much, and one said it outright. I became a silent sufferer, which made things all the worse.

These days, I'm more than happy to envision small changes that I can get done in the span of 24-48 hours, and trust that everything works out from there. And what's more, I make so much more real progress!

How powerful is the power of the small? For me, it was like discovering the energy within an atom, because when small changes are unleashed and accumulated, I discover I have set off a chain reaction with similar profound effect.

We address some aspects of the stickiness of problems, especially our habitual ones, and our attraction to them later in the book. It's interesting to know why problems get sticky, but not necessary. Using the Matrix is a short-cut for dealing with those difficult emotions because it helps you move toward healthier feelings by focusing on a solution, not the problem. Solutions, by nature, are more positive than problems.

Building confidence that small changes will accumulate into bigger changes is helpful. When we value the small changes we do make, we naturally feel better. If you want to more fully understand the enormous difference small changes does make, take a quick read of Malcolm Gladwell's "Tipping Point: How little things can make a big difference."

Still, you might ask, "Really? Small changes make all the difference?" Yes, and there's really no other way around it. If you are waiting for the mountain to come to you, then you will never, ever make the first steps to getting to its foothills, much less climbing it.

However, if you take a few steps out your front door, your perspective of the world changes, even if only a tiny bit. If you take a walk around the neighborhood, your perspective changes even more. If you travel to another part of the globe, the change becomes even more dramatic. The point is, you have to take those first steps.

The fact that small changes lead to bigger changes confronts us, but it can also motivate and free us

---

You might indeed be overwhelmed by a big problem and feel trapped by it. Even so, you are always free to do small things that may not solve the problem, but will solve your feeling of being trapped.

You are free to change the thoughts in your mind. You are free to change one thing, any thing, each and every day. Do one thing, then do another. See how they work, or don't. Change this, change that. Check in with someone to see if they notice the changes you have made. If they haven't, don't worry, just keep making small changes. They will eventually notice and the reason is simple. Those small changes will add up. Plus, you might discover that making small changes is fun rather than dreadful, exciting and no longer traumatic!

This is hopeful, right? Yes, it is! It seems so evident, but remember that we seem to naturally resist change, even the small ones we really can make. We think it's because we have been so convinced of Big Mistake #2, that difficult problems need complicated solutions, that the mere thought of trying to change the problem overwhelms us.

But, that's our point. Forget about the problem. Seriously. We mean it. We'll repeat it. You'll get used to it. In fact, we'll repeat it right now. Forget about how big the problem is, and focus on one small change you can make today. Now!

Even if it's as simple as, hmm, forgetting about the problem for the next few minutes. Try something a little outrageous (?) such as going outside and hugging a tree (yes, even if you are not the Greenpeace kind!). If it's cold outside, you might discover that big old tree has a surprising warmth to it. Perhaps the bark is rough on your cheek or strangely smooth. Perhaps a full moon shines through the leaves revealing the red of your shirt and that you can the colors so clearly at one in the morning surprises you. Who knows what you will discover!

Breathe in and out slowly and deeply, think for a moment what that tree may have seen in it's lifetime. Just change it up somehow! Then, go back inside and see how the rest of the day turns out. It won't make all the difference in the world, but it will make a small change, and who knows what will happen next.

If you don't feel like going outside, or can't for other reasons, sit up straight where you are. Relax and take a few deep breaths. Close your eyes, and "lean in" (meaning, engage the moment fully without distraction). Imagine that in this moment, the problem has gone away. Allow yourself to feel what it's like to not have that %$#! problem in your life. Feel what this moment of release is like in your body.

It's rather nice, isn't it? Okay, the problem is still there, but for that moment, it wasn't. You can do that several times a day, take a break from the problem and let your mind and body experience the relief.

The fact that small changes lead to bigger changes confronts us, but it can also motivate us, and in short, free us. Again, feel free to change one small thing right now, even if it has *nothing* to do with your problem! Why wait until you finish this book? Change your life right where you are, right now!

Marilyn

Why do we urge you to get started before you've even read the first lesson? Before I delved into her system, Karen once advised me to hug a tree. She knew full well that I'm not a tree hugger, which is precisely why she instructed me to do it. To my surprise, I heeded her advice, even though it seemed wacky (again, exactly why she advised it).

I went on an afternoon hike, found a suitable tree and hugged it. Did my whole life change? No, but taking a walk in the fresh air, along a lovely stream did something for my state of mind. In the calm of that autumn afternoon, I finally came to a crucial decision that had been churning in my mind and heart for years.

The key lesson of this principle is to never, and we mean not ever, underestimate the power of the small. When we think, "Oh, that's not going to work on this big horrible problem," we are just giving ourselves an excuse to do nothing. That's fine if you like big horrible problems hanging onto your neck like an 800-pound gorilla for the rest of your life. But, if you would prefer them a little less clingy, this principle is one you just can't afford to avoid.

---

3. Change in our own sphere of influence naturally (and inexorably) affects change in others

---

When we are confronted with some of our most difficult problems, we are usually faced with the behavior of others—a person, group, community, government—that we deem as impossible. Simply put, *they* are not cooperating with our current desires. What's worse, we become convinced that *they* are never going to change.

There is an adage that reveals how ineffective it is to only want others to change: "Resentment is like drinking poison and hoping the other person dies." But, let's be honest, focusing on how we want others to change is a very good way to avoid the work of changing ourselves.

The long and short of this principle is that it redirects us back to the one and only person we can truly change. And when we do make those changes, we are re-infused with a confidence in our ability to effect change.

While we have bosses, at work, but elsewhere, too, none of them are actually *the* boss over our inner personal lives, our individual decisions about how to get through each day.

The more we realize how our choices impact our own lives, as well as others, the more empowered we are to make them. Part of the problem of problems is that we end up feeling disempowered, believing that we have no choice and that whatever we do is meaningless. The only thing that is meaningless is doing nothing.

It's true that we cannot control every aspect of our lives. And even truer that we cannot control aspects of another person's life. But, we can impact the area of our lives that we identify as our sphere of influence.

Karen

Why do I say we *do* influence everything? It's simple physics. Everything we do, directly or indirectly impacts everything else in the cosmos, although that influence in most cases, may be infinitesimally small. Sometimes, even these small changes, especially in the initial stages of a process can facilitate unexpected large changes. This kind of pivotal change has been popularized as the "butterfly effect."

When we recognize the inevitability of change, the real issue shifts from "Don't I make a difference?" to "What difference do I *want* to make?"

This is for some a huge conceptual shift. It helps us change our focus away from our inability to make a difference to, "How am I going to make the kind of difference I want to make?"

Now that is a different conversation with enormously different outcomes. Okay, okay so you might not be able to directly influence someone high up in the corporation for which you work. But the chances are, even if they did do exactly what you wanted, there would be other people/teams/organizations/laws/policies that you also want to change. And while it may be surprising, it just might be the person sitting in your cubicle who happens to be the best one to make the greatest change *consistent with the kind of change you want to see*!

By "owning" your ideas and insights, you can decide if your organization and those you are working with are really worth the effort it will take to effect the change. Sure, we would like it to be easier; we would like having life served to us on a silver platter. But, life doesn't even happen for the rich and famous that way!

Here are two scenarios taken from the lives of real, ordinary people that illustrate our point:

Scenario One: You dislike the job you currently have, but may not be able to change it right away. However, there is nothing stopping you from looking for a more optimal job. Until you find one, you continue to do the best you can in the meantime. With the subtle release of stress brought about by your internal decision, your co-workers comment that in the past few days, you've become less critical in general and more approachable. They appreciate your newfound sense of hope, even though they do not know you have made a decision to someday leave that particular environment.

Scenario Two: Despite significant challenges at work, you determine that the mission and goals of your organization are worth the time and effort to stay. You make whatever changes you can to keep your job bearable. While you know your changes do not directly effect change in the people above you, they seem to have an effect on people right around you.

In the meantime, you study more about institutional change and come to some realizations about the organization you work for. You accept that your corporation is unlikely to change in the way that you desire, but you also have formulated a plan that will effect a few small changes, and could later be adopted in a larger context at work.

Your decisions will be guided by your own self-knowledge, clarity of your sense of mission and capacities and the like. But in the beginning, the issue is not whether you can make a difference, but what kind of difference you want to make, and that is what determines your course of action from there.

Joe (not his real name), a student

As (Joe) explored the issue, Karen asked him what he would like to change at work. At first, he fumed a long litany of complaints, the gist of it being how he wanted his boss to change. When Karen finally got a word in edgewise, she asked, "And what would you like to change in yourself, in this situation?"

Joe paused and quietly admitted he hadn't thought of what he could change, so fixated upon the unacceptable things his boss was doing. He had simply not looked in the most obvious place where changes can happen the fastest–his own actions. A few days later, he responded to that question with this scenario.

"I decided to change how I reacted when my boss made the next unreasonable demand on me. Instead of getting mad, I calmly told him I would try to do my best, and didn't promise anything else. I then tried to stay relaxed while completing the task, which took a couple days.

"When I handed the work in, I remained non-committed to his response. He was going to say whatever he wanted anyway, so I just gave it to him without my usual excuses as to why I thought it wasn't perfect. Somehow, I think my relaxed attitude may have helped him be a little less critical, which is what we all have come to expect from him. And then, when he did criticize my work, I just said that I'd fix it up for him and left it at that. I kept my emotions unattached."

Karen asked if his boss had changed at all. Joe replied that he had not, from what he could see. Then Karen asked if anything was different at work. He thought for a moment and replied, "You know what? Yeah. I'm less uptight. I got to thinking that since he hasn't fired me or anyone else at this point, he probably just says that as a way of motivating us. We don't like it, but maybe that's the only way he knows how to run an office, so I'm just going to keep shrugging it off. If he does fire me, I'll cross that bridge when I come to it."

Already, Joe's experience at work was different. His boss had not changed all that much, but Joe's reaction to his boss' comments had. This is one small example of how making changes in our *own* life can improve our circumstances even if the other person makes no changes to accommodate us.

Now do I detect a little disappointment that the changes Joe made didn't result in his boss having an epiphany that he should find Joe and beg his forgiveness for the way he had been mistreating him?

Sometimes, what we want is not change, per se, but rather some kind of payback for whatever suffering we perceive the other has caused us. That's self-justification at best and a subtle form of revenge (wanting the other to eat humble pie) at worst.

All that we are advocating here is to make changes within your sphere of influence. And then, see what happens. This system is not about forcing you, nor those in your life, to do anything, other than what is helpful to you.

On the clinical side of this genre, *"Solutions focusing is not solutions forcing,"* is a commonly used reminder. You'll see it more than once in this book as well.

When you focus your changes, those small, doable changes, upon your immediate surroundings, your results are much more likely to be experienced quickly. This will boost your sense of accomplishment and likewise your self-confidence to effect even more changes.

And someday, who knows? Those changes may go all the way past your boss to his/her boss and even beyond. But, at the very least, in the meantime, you'll be a more pleasant person to work with. That's not a bad thing.

Principles of Investment

4. You invest in what you create

How many times have you given someone just the best piece of advice ever? Quite possibly the answer is, 'Lots of times to lots of people." And, did they follow those golden nuggets of wisdom? Not so much. If your family and friends are anything like mine, they listened to your advice with polite attention and then proceeded to handle things in their own way.

But, let's be fair and turn that around. How many times has someone given you advice, and how closely did you follow it? I'm sure there were times when you took in another's opinion and made good use of it.

I'm also sure there is a lot of great information and detailed instruction you've heard or read from diet experts, relationship counselors, career consultants and the like, all to whom you've paid little or no heed.

It's well known that people tend to take better care of what they own. This doesn't mean apartment dwellers aren't responsible. Most are, but when they become house owners, they are usually more diligent about their property. It's the same with advice. We can easily give it, and just as easily ignore it. However, when we invest in creating our own solutions, we tend to pay more attention to the plan we devise.

This is especially true when we ask the right kind of questions that lead us to solutions, especially when broken down into doable steps that we're relatively confident to achieve. Even rocket science, in each particular detail, is achieved one simple step after another. All together, constructing a space shuttle is indeed complicated, but not necessarily each step of it.

In this way, when you construct your own solution, it becomes your own ship to sail to whatever destination you desire. Will you ignore your own advice? Maybe. But then again, if you set aside your own plan, your are more likely to later to pick it up again when you're readier to implement it.

When you create your own solution, it is much more likely to accurately address your problem, because no one can experience your problem in quite the way that you do.

This point is rather simple and does not need much belaboring. When you create your own solution, it is much more likely to accurately address your problem, because no one can experience your problem in quite the way that you do. This means that while their advice might be good, it might not be the most fitting path for you to follow. And this takes us directly to the next principle.

5. You are the expert of your life

Don't let anyone ever convince you otherwise. Anyone who tells you they know you better than you know yourself is flat out wrong. And if you believe them, you just might be, too. When explaining how this principle works in her Solutions Mastery System, Karen likes to use a formula made famous by Abe Lincoln in his Gettysburg address: "The best chance for a solution to work is when we create if *of* ourselves, *by* ourselves and *for* ourselves."

Here's how she breaks it down in her online course:

Of ourselves means that we create solutions from the stuff of our lives, the experience of and connection to others that has informed and invigorated us. It means that we create a solution devised from our better intuitions, thoughts, feelings and deeper convictions.

By ourselves means that we use and rely upon our own creative capacities, and not depend upon others to tell us what to do. This does not mean we never seek advice from others. Of course, it's good to consider other points of view. That gives us perspective. However, when it comes to creating a solution for the particular problem you are engaging, at the end of the day, your best bet is your own self.

Leaning on others is good for temporary support, but eventually, this is your life to have and hold. It can be scary, especially if you've dug yourself into a rather deep hole, but it is also exciting (c'mon, just a little, isn't it?). It is not always simple, but it is profoundly regenerative when you begin to take back pieces of your life and make them uniquely your own again.

For ourselves means that we design solutions that fit our lives, specifically created to adjust to our style, and meant to work at pace with who we are, mentally, emotionally, physically. No matter how wonderful a solution might be, if it doesn't *fit* us, we will eventually discard it.

"If I had an hour to solve a problem and my life depended on the solution, I would spend the first 55 minutes determining the proper question to ask, for once I know the proper question, I could solve the problem in less than five minutes."
—Albert Einstein

It's helpful to remember, that being the expert of our life doesn't mean there is nothing left to learn, nor others to learn from. So what does it mean then that we are the expert of our life?

It means that no one else can know what is truly meaningful and what matters most to *us*. These are the defining qualities that we hold nearest and dearest to our hearts, the real truth about who we are and what we want.

The Solutions Mastery System doesn't give you answers to everything you ask. It's more useful than that. It provides you with ways to ask the right questions that lead *you* to the answers *you* need in order to create workable solutions for *your* life. That's it in a nutshell. These principles are reassurances that you have the right stuff within you, and that this right stuff is readily available to you so that you can make the changes you want in your life.

6. You have the resources and resilience

You are creative. Yes, you are. It doesn't matter if you can't paint a masterpiece or play concert piano. We all have imaginations. It's entirely doable for you to find a few minutes in your day where you can quietly sit with your eyes closed and imagine your life without the problem in it.

You will be amazed at what you can imagine yourself doing, which is usually whatever you truly want to do, but have come to believe the problem prevents you from doing. Yes, you have to come back down to reality, smack dab in the middle of where that pesky problem pervades, but the point is, you don't have to live with it every single moment of the day and night in your head.

However, the critical point of this Principle is that when you more accurately claim your expertise over your life, you are more capable of then informing others of your real hopes, dreams and day-to-day goals.

Further, you are resilient. After all, you're here, reading this book, and this means you've survived another day with "that damn spot" in your life. So, you have come this far. You're amazing! We don't mean this lightly. We all encounter problems, even Karen readily admits to that (though she prefers to think of them as challenges).

You, we, don't lack anything. It's just that we often forget who we are, so busy focusing on being all that others want us to be. That's somewhat okay, and truly understandable, but we really do have to focus on who we are, and what we really want.

This doesn't make us selfish people. In fact, when you discover more accurately who you are and what you want, you will very likely rediscover that you are a good person who wants what is best for yourself and others. Otherwise, you wouldn't be seeking to improve yourself through a self-help book, now would you?

However, the critical point of this Principle is that when you more accurately claim your expertise over your life, you become more capable of informing others of your real hopes, dreams and day-to-day goals. In fact, they are likely to appreciate knowing more fully who you are and what you want, so long as your expectation is not for them to deliver those aspirations to you. This system is about dealing with reality, after all.

7. You want to get better and are doing the best you can

I know, you are thinking, "If that's true, then why can't I get out of this pile of crap I seem to be forever stuck in?" It might be because you are a member of the human species. Get over it. The truth is that all but the rare human being wants to become a better version of themselves, improve their lot in life and have better relationships with others.

Yes, your life, and in fact the whole world may be a mess, but we humans keep trying to make things better. It may look like we're not doing the best we can, but the United Nations is just one indication that we continue to step forward, that we long for something better than the good old days of Genghis Khan and his marauding hordes.

Sometimes it just takes us a little longer than we would like, or requires us to take different paths than we at first thought were possible or desirable.

All right, you might be knee deep in a stinking mess right now, but you've been doing the best you could do given all that has been going on in your life to this point. Anyone else in your exact situation would quite possibly not have fared so well!

Honestly, you are halfway there when you accept that you want to be a better version of yourself *and* that, remarkably, you've already been doing enormously well with what you've had available to you. Leave the blame and shame game and language behind. It's obsolete.

The past cannot be changed. If you've been immoral and unethical in the past, focus on the future you want. If you continue to dwell on the past and feel bad about yourself, you will find it difficult to make those changes that will help you live more honestly.

The System is a simple method that answers, "How do I do that?" When you leverage this one new insight, "Focus on solutions not on problems" you will begin to "live your life forward." Plus, accepting that you were doing the best you could, given whatever circumstances you were in, you can begin the necessary process of healing.

Why is this principle important?

It is counter-intuitive to most that someone with a problem may actually be performing exceptionally. But it's an important aspect to acknowledge and value. Let's look at something in that line that we already know and value: our bodies' ability to heal.

When we have an injury or get a virus or infection, while we feel sick, perhaps in serious pain, we rely on our body's innate ability to heal. Our bodies are absolute marvels of creation. We don't know how we do it, but our bodies work very hard to heal.

When we engage in an injurious relationship or get hit with an illness, we too, naturally seek to heal. Sure, sometimes we get sidelined and meet other complications, but it is nevertheless important to know that all this while something marvelous is taking place.

We are also striving to heal our situations, and from these less-than-optimal situations, are doing our best. We work with what we have, and quite frankly, often do miracles. It is important to acknowledge and realize that we have a lot going for us, even when the chips are down.

What all the problem-focused people in your life have not helped you realize is that you've done a remarkable job up to now, considering you've been up against a wall that seemed too high to get over, too wide to get around and too thick to knock a hole through to the other side.

To get here, you've been enormously resourceful and resilient. Now it's time to use all that great stuff that has kept you upright, even while against the wall, in small creative ways that will get you over, around, or through it. If you can't imagine any way up, around or through the wall, but figure out how to dig a tunnel under it, we would only say, "You go for it!"

Principles of Solutions

There are actually a few more of these, but the following are the essential ones that we think help you the most when applying the System.

*We promised to repeat this,
so here it is again*

8. You do not need to know anything about a problem in order to create an effective solution for it

This principle is just so liberating! We have for so long paid homage to our problems, that it's hard to turn our backs on them. But think about it for a minute. Even if we do turn our backs on the problem and start to pay attention to other things in life, (say for instance, to creating solutions), why would that be problematic? Do we really have to keep engaging with our problems in order to create a situation in which that problem is no longer happening? The answer is simply, "No!"

We just have a long history of intimate relationships with our problems, so much so that we develop a kind of Stockholm syndrome toward them. We begin to defend the existence of the problem in our life, in the same way that some hostages will defend and identify with their captors. We can become so identified with our problems that we barely recognize ourselves without them.

We understand the attraction that problems have for us and it's helpful to be aware that you may have been, and most likely will be again, seduced by the complexity of your problems. Why do we cling so arduously to our problems?

Suffice it to say that when we take our problems to others, we often get sympathy. We're wired from birth to appreciate sympathy. When we're babies and our tummies tell us we're hungry, we cry. Voila! Mom feeds us. Yum. When our diaper is wet, we cry. Hey! Dad changes it. Nice.

No wonder then, as other problems that pertain to an adult's life press upon us, we tend to seek sympathy. We aren't suggesting you not confide in trusted friends, or a qualified therapist if need be. What we are suggesting is that, at the end of the day, sympathy is not a *solution*.

Sympathy is comforting, and there is certainly nothing wrong with that. But, don't confuse all the time spent getting comfort with being anything like the art and craft of creating solutions in your life.

At the end of the day, we all have to get down to business and figure out the changes we need to make in order to clear a path through the confusion in which we find ourselves. And it is the Matrix (coming up soon) that gives you that compass to guide your next steps when the pain of your biggest problems hangs like a thick, heavy fog over you.

9. Exceptions indicate solutions

No problem is ongoing every second of our waking and sleeping lives, though they may seem to be. There are moments in most days when the problem isn't happening. Some days the problem doesn't occur at all. Have you noticed what's going on when *the problem isn't happening*?

We rarely look closely enough at these exceptions to the problem because we are so focused on all that's going on when the problem *is* happening. However, these exceptions are enormously helpful because they tell us a lot about where our solutions to a particular problem might lay. Taking the time to investigate exceptions, to recall what we were doing when the problem was **not** happening allows us to understand that we already have some pieces of a blueprint for the solution of that problem, going forward. Pretty cool, huh?

The other way of saying this is, "Success leaves clues." So when you successfully have a day, or an hour or even a few minutes when the problem is not happening, look carefully around to see where you are, what you are doing, who you are with, your frame of mind, the words you use, and so on.

Look for what you know you already do that works, even a little. Now you are really on to something!

---

10. The simplest and least invasive approach is usually the best medicine

---

Remember Mary Poppins? She's the nanny who advised that a spoonful of sugar helps the medicine go down. In this case, the sugar is simplicity. This principle is closely linked to how small changes lead to bigger changes. Trying to create complicated solutions is just, well, how can we say it nicely? It's just a near sure-fire way to make the problem worse, or create yet another problem on top of the problem we're trying to fix, is what it is. That's as nice as we can be.

Simple, small, significant. That's the way it is with solutions. It's one reason why they're not as attractive as problems: There isn't a big "ta-da" associated with them.

Not every solution has to be simple enough for a 5th grader to understand, but for the most part, that's about the level of complexity you need in order to create a truly effective one. We didn't tell you that this book would boost your ego (though practice of the Matrix will boost your self-confidence).

Often, a really good solution requires some humility. We don't mean humility in the sense of self-deprecation. We're not fond of that habit. We mean humility in the sense of honest self-assessment. Knowing that the simplest and least invasive way is best when we're effecting changes in our lives helps us be more honest about who we are and what we really want in our lives.

It helps us keep our self-talk simple, direct, clear. It's all the complicated stuff we tell ourselves (rationalizations) that often gets us, and keeps us, in trouble.

Simple, small, significant. That's the way it is with solutions. It's one reason why they're not as attractive as problems: There isn't a big "ta-da" associated with them.

Keeping it simple is really the wise way to go. And, when you keep your solutions simple, something else naturally happens. Joy starts to creep into areas of your life once overshadowed by those doom and gloom clouds. Keeping it simple becomes an art form, actually, a way to live with a bit of lightness in your step.

And it's a lot cheaper than a year's worth of ballroom dancing lessons! See? It's all win-win.

4. Common Sense Rules of Thumb

Solutions Rules of Thumb (SRTs) That Really Do Help

You're gonna love these 10 little rules for 10 little reasons (these are the reasons):

1. They're basic common sense (if you can count to 2 you can use 'em)
2. They're easy to understand (you don't need to be a rocket scientist)
3. They're easy to follow (even if you are a rocket scientist)
4. They're easy to explain (we're not rocket scientists and we teach this stuff)
5. They're easy to remember (or print out a pocket-reminder)
6. They're applicable (for anyone, anytime, anywhere)
7. They're trustworthy (help every time you *use* 'em)
8. They're absolutely *doable* (doable is as doable does)

9. They're encouraging (no rapped knuckles here!)
10. They're *fun*! (self explanatory)

First let's clear up any misgivings you may have about rules. If you happen to break any or all of our rules above, nothing bad will happen to you. These rules aren't here to discourage you *from doing* something, rather they're here to encourage you *to do* something, anything you find useful, helpful, enjoyable and not harmful to yourself or others.

This is self-help, not religion. Not that we're dissing religion, by the way. We are simply saying these SRTs are handy and helpful, but they are not an overarching philosophy to which you must adhere, "or else."

If you happen to apply a few or more of them, you'll truly enhance your solutions-making process, which means you'll be melting away the parameters of your problem(s) more efficiently and effectively than if you ignore them.

But, it's up to you. We certainly don't remember all 10 of them at any given time. Most of the time, we don't even think of them until we're stuck, and then one of the rules pops into our head and we smile and say, "Ah, that's what we need to do." These SRTs are like a longtime trusted friend, the kind that doesn't mind giving you a poke in the ribs from time to time, but only when you truly need it.

If you have a few "duh" moments reading these 10 SRTs, recall that we titled this chapter, "Common Sense Rules of Thumb." What good is a self-help program with instructions so complicated and goals so lofty no one can understand or follow it?

I guess we could have written a dense tome that only academes would decipher, but what's the fun in that? And when have you ever seen a philosophy professor in the aisle of any DIY or self-help genre?

Besides, it isn't *what* we know that makes a difference in our lives: It's what we **do** with what we know that makes all the difference. So, here we go with 10 little rules that will jet propel you forward, not only into the next chapters that teach you the Solutions Mastery System, but into your new life that is beckoning to you, just a few pages down the road.

1. Start at the beginning and not at the end.

Focus on how you will begin
rather than where you will end up

We have built into this rule, the use of something we call the "JumpStart2," (JS2) and we'll explain that in a moment. The main point of this rule is that we often know how we want things to be in the end, and find it very hard to believe how we'll ever get there.

Here's a very common example. Most people start a diet thinking, "I want to weigh 150 pounds when I'm done." And then, they step on the scale, look down, and all of a sudden, their DAG loop is set in motion.

Doubt rushes in like a tsunami. The goal seems so distant and undoable. They lose all motivation to do what they think will be demanded of them to get down to their desired weight. Many a diet starts and ends right there on the scale.

On the other hand, when a dieter starts out thinking, "I want to do something different today about my lack of exercise; I think I'll take a two minute walk"–they have an enormously better chance of getting up and actually taking that 2-minute walk.

That is a JS2. It's the ignition for the journey that lies ahead. Remember that small changes accumulate into bigger ones, so just get started and let the end unfold as it will. And using the JS2 makes the start absolutely doable!

You'll get used to this open-ended way of thinking when you start to put the Solutions Mastery System into use. But, suffice it to say, this is a critical rule of thumb. Every solution has a beginning, middle and an end*ing* (with an emphasis on the "ing," the ongoing part). But without a beginning, you haven't any chance of getting through the middle and making it to that ongoing end. Life, after all, is not static. Neither are our goals, so we will be constantly tweaking and adjusting them in an ongoing manner. That way we keep them fresh, alive and relevant to our constantly, magnificently changing lives!

Using the JS2 will help you overcome the king of all monkey wrenches known to flummox the works of any good solution: procrastination.

We've already mentioned how wanting change, yet dreading change can freeze us into indecision. This frozen state is where we have actually made the choice to not choose.

This forces the choice to, at some point, be made for us. The old saying, "Procrastination is my sin. It causes me much sorrow. I know I should stop doing it. In fact, I will— tomorrow!" is humorous, but it belies the truth that we cause ourselves a lot of grief by not making decisions about change before they're forced upon us.

The most difficult part of change is the first step, but if you can make just that one step, the next steps will begin to happen spontaneously, one after the other. The System recognizes this, and thus is designed to help you take that first itty-bitty step which the hardest.

Here's how to make that step less formidable. Use the JS2 method when you feel you just cannot get started on a solution. Just do something, *anything* for 2 minutes. That's it. Set aside 1-2-minutes and do something. Do *anything*.

It doesn't have to be related to the solution you're working on. Doodle on a pad. Pretend you're a tap dancer, or grab a broom and waltz through your living room with it. Laugh the scales (a singing technique where you "ha, ha, ha," up and down a major scale).

After 2 minutes, stop and take a breath. Wasn't so bad, was it? Still stuck? Do another JS2 to spark your creative juices. Sometimes we do several for about 10-15 minutes. You'd be amazed how it just loosens you up. The sillier and funnier your JS2 is, the better effect it seems to have.

How effective is this little trick? Some writers use it every morning. They wake up and write whatever comes to mind for 2-3 minutes on a blank page. Then, they take a shower. They've stimulated their brain, but haven't seriously taxed it so that later, when they sit down to write, they are much less likely to suffer writer's block.

Marilyn

I have used this technique a lot, and most recently in writing this chapter of the book. I got behind schedule for several good reasons, but I sill felt bad. Because I felt bad about getting behind schedule, I kept avoiding the task, which was the Rules of Thumb chapter.

Each time I put it off, I felt a bit guilty. Finally, I said to myself, "You know what? This has become a problem and it needs a quick solution." This meant, I had to start at the beginning, not the end of the solution. Instead of thinking how the book was going to ever get completed (the desired end result), I decided to just start writing again, for 2 minutes. "Just 2 minutes," I told myself. I knew that I could easily write for 2 minutes. So, I sat down, took a few deep, slow breaths, picked up my computer and something happened.

Can you guess what that was? If you surmised that I wrote for much longer than 2 minutes, until I had the rough draft of this chapter completed, you would be right.

2. If it is working, do more of it

Focus On What's Going Right!

Not everything you are doing is wrong. Even folks in the worst situations really are doing some things right, even though it may not feel like it at the time.

Marilyn

I've mentioned my marriage and divorce in prior chapters. My ex was and remains a good guy. We started with the best of intentions, as newlyweds do. Unfortunately, several years into the marriage, we began to see that we were thoroughly incompatible. We had underestimated our differences, thinking that what we held in common would be enough to conquer any obstacle. We paid dearly for this inaccurate assessment.

The relationship deteriorated into daily argument, and at first we compromised, but both of us begrudged doing so. Our resentments grew, layer by layer, and new disagreements dredged up what we thought we had settled in previous clashes. I'm not proud of this, but we both tended to keep score, and this was complicated by different point systems. In other words, what he thought were major offenses seemed minor to me, and vice versa.

Things kept getting worse no matter how hard we tried to work it out. Eventually, after the kids matured and become independent, we separated. We both felt deeply about what we were doing, and our regret was profound. However, in the separation, we found ways to converse in a civil manner, to the point where we forged a respectful friendship. This remains the state of our relationship and I enjoy hearing from him when he calls, as I hope he does when I give him a ring.

The point is, not everything we did was wrong. We may not have had enough to sustain a lifelong marital bond, but there were a few things we got right, and could continue to do. And these few things we don't try to fix because they work for us, as friends.

So, the couple in the illustration above discovered that not everything they did was wrong, and they continued to develop the few things they were doing right. Although they did not "save" their marriage, they did find ways to begin and maintain a friendship, which is a far cry better than what most ex-couples are able to achieve.

The takeaway from this Rule of Thumb is that when we begin to use the Matrix, and especially the line of inquiry that uses positive recall, we focus on the past only to draw from it what was going right. It may be one small good thing in a pile of awful things, but nonetheless, that's the thing we focus on.

Solutions focusing is not about weighing the good and the bad in our lives. It is not that kind of an assessment tool. If you need to do that, to judge whether you are an overall good or bad person, that's something you need to do, but you don't need to use the Matrix in that kind of exercise.

When it comes to devising solutions, you look for what went right in previous times in order to bring that right thing forward into either the same problem area, or a different one. Because, if something is working for you, doing more of it makes sense.

Likewise, the next Rule of Thumb, the opposite of this one, makes the same kind of sense. Let's take a look at that now.

3. If it isn't working, try something else.

Stop Digging!

Duh, if ever there was a duh! But, this has to be emphasized because there's another saying that seems to predominate our performance driven culture, "If you at first don't succeed, try, try again."

This is solid advice if you want to develop muscle memory, such as getting that new dance step down. But, it is not a viable tactic for resolving a problem, because doing the same thing that led to the problem is not going to help you to leave the problem behind.

Sometimes, doing something different is very basic. It may mean not trying anything at all, as in not trying to make the other to think, feel or do what we want them to think, feel or do.

> *Doing one small thing differently yourself, however, opens a window that allows for a bit of sunlight and fresh air to enter the situation.*

But, more often, doing something different is just that. If shouting at your teenager no longer works, you should probably stop shouting. Inform them that shouting has done no good and you will whisper from now on. At the least, you will save your voice and they might become intrigued by what you are whispering and listen more closely. You won't know until you try.

In other words, we give you permission to stop digging the same hole over and over. In fact, you can put up that problem-oriented shovel and stop digging altogether.

---

4. Keep it simple.

Positive. Practical. Present.

We really do mean this. If you use the Matrix and start making up complicated steps to achieve your goals, good luck, but don't blame us if you find yourself not succeeding.

Yes, problems are often complex, difficult, sticky, messy and fraught with hard decisions that we'd rather not have to make. Your solutions, however, do not have to be hard or complicated. They can be as easy as a JS2.

How hard is it to do something for 2 minutes? Not very hard! How much harder is it to do something for 2 hours? With our busy modern day schedules, it's hard to find an extra 20 minutes in which to get something done.

But, a 2-minute solution? It's downright embarrassing if you avoid that. So, make each step of your solution something you know you can do, and build on it from there as needed.

Yes, we know this is such a common sense thing to say. However, when we are dealing with difficulties, we tend to think in an anxious frame of mind. We tend to respond to problems in two ways nearly polar opposite of each other, neither of which work very well.

The first is avoidance. We convince ourselves that maybe the whole thing will disappear on its own. Or, we lay the onus of change on others. Or, we make the problem into "God almighty" and say it's so overwhelming we might as well not even try. These are all "flight" responses.

The second way is to charge forward head-on and hope that if we yell and stomp loud and hard enough, the problem will turn tail and run from us. When a problem arises that causes emotional conflict in us, we sometimes reach for anger as a means to deal with it. This is the classic "fight" response.

Keeping it simple helps you avoid either end of this spectrum. You don't have to hide from your problem. If you keep your solution steps simple, you know you are more likely to actually do them. This gives you some confidence at the start, and you will then be less likely to avoid what confronts you.

Accomplishing even small victories has the welcome impact of letting yourself feel better about yourself, and others in general, often to a surprisingly large degree. Plus you tend to react less, because you're planning and effecting changes more, and your interest zeros in more on that. You more readily reach for your doable solutions, and react less and less with frustration and anger.

So, try "simple," and keep it that way.

It's just that simple.

5. Focus on strengths and resources, not on weaknesses and deficits.

You Are Resourceful & Resilient

It sounds so obvious, but when you listen to everyday conversations or read the news, weaknesses and deficits certainly take the marquee. We not only point out others' faults, but often shame ourselves with, "How did I get myself into this mess?"

We also blame: "What's wrong with them?" "What's wrong with me?" We feel mad, bad, sad and stupid, often lashing out from embarrassment. We let the problem define who we are. We call ourselves names, such as "addict" or "fool" or "failure" or worse.

We say things to ourselves that we wouldn't allow others to say to our face. Our self-talk becomes a type of mental pollution. We allow our trash-talk "dirt" to pile up or even stick it on the walls of our thoughts like bad poster art. Were such words and phrases actual mud on our bodies, we'd be sure to wash it off as soon as we could get to a shower.

It's odd how many of us have poor mental hygiene habits. We say these hurtful things to ourselves, over and over, convincing ourselves that it's all so very true. And worse, we go to sleep in that muddied state, never giving our mind a chance to feel clean. Few of us would tolerate our partner or spouse climbing into bed next to us with dirty feet, or un-brushed teeth, but we don't think once about cleaning up our self-talk.

What is the overall tone of your inner world?

A Princeton psychology professor, Dr. Amy Cuddy, did a study on body posture and discovered that people can significantly boost self-confidence by standing for two-minutes (yep, that's all it takes) in the "Wonder Woman" or "Superman" pose. We've all seen it, and many of us have probably done it when we were kids

Dr. Cuddy's research found that those who did this simple exercise before engaging in a graduate class discussion entered into the conversation and responded with more assertive answers than did their counterparts who were asked to sit slouched in a chair prior to a similar assignment.

Her own story is rather remarkable, and worth telling in this context. She had been a very bright student, but suffered brain damage in a car accident, enough to alter her overall I.Q. She was told by more than one expert that it was no longer likely for her to get through college.

Instead of focusing on the weaknesses and deficits incurred from this accident, she decided that she had enough capacity to keep going, even though she would now need tutors and a longer period of time to accomplish her goal of obtaining a bachelor's degree. It did take her several more years, but she managed.

Eventually, she went even further. She went through graduate school and became a doctoral candidate. Although she was slowly climbing the academic ladder, what she had heard from the experts lingered in her mind. She kept thinking to herself, "I don't belong here."

One day, she said those words out loud to her advisor who responded with, "Then fake it until you make it. You *do* belong here. You've convinced me of that. Now, you just have to convince yourself."

She took that advice to heart, and in the very next class pushed herself to jump into the discussion where before she would have remained silent. To her surprise, no one told her that her idea was wrong or stupid. In fact, a few of the students said her concept was novel and quite good.

This isn't to encourage you to lie, cheat or otherwise fool people. Dr. Cuddy's advisor wasn't telling her to be inauthentic. She believed in her student, and all that she wanted was the student to believe in herself. She knew that if she didn't get involved in the class discussions, she would never develop the confidence to go on.

The point is, if you focus on your strengths, and look around at the good resources available to you, rather than continue to belittle yourself and ignore helpful persons who have your interests at heart, you will find it much easier to develop a good solution.

There is a bonus. As we notice our own good qualities, we then tend to notice good things in those around us. If you've been a habitual self-critical fault-finder, this self-talk sneaks out into what you think, and sometimes say, about others. Eventually, it becomes a way of life.

As you develop a more loving self-dialogue, you will begin to see the strengths and resources in others, and call upon them to work with you in a collegial manner. They'll want to do so because it's fun to work with assertive, affirming, positive people.

There is a reason the "Golden Rule" is found in nearly every religion, large or small. What have you to lose by loving yourself and your neighbors, whomever and wherever they may be? Focusing upon your strengths and resources is just another way to love yourself, which is okay. Really.

You will discover things about yourself from long ago that you had forgotten about. And, as you focus on what you do have, rather than what you lack, you will begin to feel you have an abundant life, not a meager one.

You will begin to share your good stuff with others, and they will feel as if they can share their good stuff with you. It's the opposite kind of loop from the DAG loop we've talked about earlier. We could call it the "rise and shine" loop. In fact, we just have.

6. Look forward, not back.

After All, We're All Headed There.

How often do we use this rule of thumb? Every day. Sometimes hourly, and in difficult situations, minute by minute. Not a one of us can say we look back on life without any regrets. We all have them. Here's the problem with keeping our focus on those regrets. We cannot do one single thing to change the past. Not one single thing. Not ever.

It's all right to be aware of the past, and better to learn from it. And, it's really great when you can change the course of your present and future because of what you've learned. Although we all do it, we have to remind you, as well as ourselves, that it is a waste of precious time to look back and long for the past to be different.

Sadly we can't bag up our past and take those bits and pieces like old clothes to a thrift store. The thoughts in our heads are less like articles of clothing and more like familiar ghosts. They don't stay where we put them.

Instead, they drift through the corridors of our minds, old thoughts and feelings always ready to visit, again and again.

This is actually a wonderful thing about the human brain. Once it has something imprinted into it, it tends to stay. And amazingly, like a Jack-in-the-Box, those memories pop up with just the slightest of nudges.

This ability to access memories so we can do things without occupying the mind with the low-level details required, allows us to develop automatic response patterns, better known as habits that help us complete repetitive tasks like tying shoes.

This automaticity (as it is referred to in neuroscience) is an essential aspect of learning and creating as we add new information upon old, sifting and sorting our way through life with an efficiency that would otherwise be impossible if we had to continually relearn the old.

Looking forward, not back, means that when those memories do arise, we acknowledge them, but do not follow them like a rabbit down the hole. We kindly but firmly shift our mind's eye and focus instead on what we *can* do from that moment onward.

We understand this is harder to do for some because they haven't yet disconnected the emotional impulses from those memories.

To listen to and lean into our fears, but not let them ride off with us, is a skill we can learn for everyday issues. Some may well need professional help in freeing them from unhealthy triggers associated with Post Traumatic Stress Disorder for example. Most of us simply need to be self aware, and when we find ourselves going back over an old problem, remind ourselves to "Stop that ball," and focus instead on what we can do going forward.

We can accelerate some emotions and decelerate others. Reminding ourselves to "shift our direction of focus" and to look forward rather than back is akin to developing any habit. We have to practice it over a period of time until it becomes more or less a default.

Sheena (not her real name), a student

When I completed my first yoga class, my thigh muscles complained vociferously the next day. I didn't want to go back to the second class, but I'm glad that I did. It took a few classes until my body began to feel better about the odd contortions I was asking it to perform.

Each time the instructor taught us a new stance, my body resisted at first. It liked the old complacent way of not stretching those muscles. It complained, but eventually, those muscles learned the new stance.

Yoga did not become my favorite form of exercise. The point was not to become its poster girl. The point was for my body to learn something new, and now that it has, when I go to a class, I slip right into this new mode of standing, bending, turning and sitting.

Your brain will be the same. Some parts will almost ache as you stop fixating on the past and instead look to what lies ahead. With time, you find yourself shaking off the "old haunts" as quickly as they waft through the rafters to spook you. And you'll be amazed at how compliant they become to your request to let you focus on what you need to do going forward.

The more you experience looking forward with curiosity as to what is about to happen, the less the past has a hold on you. It's just that simple, but it does take some practice. Like a new yoga student, your brain will feel awkward about not looking back, but over time, it does get used to the new ways of looking forward.

Trust us. No, better yet, trust yourself. The next time you catch yourself dwelling on the past, gently shake your head and say "Hm, wonder what's next today?" And then think about the very next thing you are going to do. Don't try to envision yourself 5 years from now.

Look forward into your immediate future. Check your grocery list or look up a movie you read good reviews about. Think about anything, just not the past. Stop yourself from entering that old DAG loop, and step into the rest of the day.

Just as our bodies process food for energy and nutrition and then release the processed remnants, being able to process our emotions fully is important to our emotional health and fitness.

Don't get us wrong. There are appropriate times to think about the past. We even guide you to constructively do so when we get to key parts of the Solutions Matrix. Honest self-reflection is different from wallowing around in the pain of the past.

Again, if your past is still causing you trauma, seek professional help and/or a support group to assist you. Our point is not to discourage anyone from seeking needed therapies, medical or psychological.

What we want you to do less of is dwell in the past with only a negative perspective. For example, there's nothing wrong with looking back at the good times to buoy us when we feel a little down.

Just as our bodies process food for energy and nutrition and then release the processed remnants, being able to process our emotions, the full range of them, glad, mad, bad, sad, is important to our emotional health and fitness. When we do so, our lives are enriched.

Looking forward, not back, does not mean we ignore the past. In fact, there is a very constructive way to look back. What this Rule of Thumb means is that we don't stay stuck in our past, suffering some kind of "emotional constipation."

We recognize there is Post Traumatic Stress, but there is also Post Traumatic Growth, and this program can be useful for those seeking a way forward in their lives.

Solutions cannot be applied in the past. They might use helpful hints and clues from the past, but it is futile to construct a solution as a means of changing the past.

The good news is that when you spend your time and energy focused on the present with a solution focused attitude, you are naturally looking forward because solutions are what lay out there in front of you. They are the next steps you plan to take for whatever effects of a problem you want to alter.

7. No single approach works for everyone.

You Are Unique. So Will Be Your Solutions.

If you had a hammer, you'd hammer in the morning, you'd hammer in the evening, all over this land. Oh, please! You can't use the same hammer for every kind of nail. There is a big difference between a roofing nail and a tiny brad.

Marilyn

Several years ago, a bit of carpet had worked its way loose along the sideboard in our basement rec room. I grabbed a regular sized hammer and a couple of small nails to secure it back down. I was successful with the first two, and just as it occurred to me they were such tiny nails and the hammer much too large for the task, I whacked my forefinger. That's a painful lesson I've never forgotten.

The same is true for problems and the people who have them. Sure, many problems are the same, but no two people ever are. That's why this book doesn't try to solve problems for *you*. We have no idea about the problems you are facing and how they affect you.

We feel fortunate that we can at least address our own. However, what we can help you with is finding solutions. We know it sounds odd that the problems don't matter all that much.

Problems do matter, but not when it comes down to devising a solution, and it's just that simple. The solution need not have anything to do with the problem, per se. It just needs to be a step in the right direction for you.

Hammer, screwdriver, pliers, are all part of a basic toolkit, and each is helpful for the many type of tasks that require them. In the same way, the Solutions Mastery System, in particular the Matrix, provides you with a few very helpful tools that can be applied to many kinds of solutions needed to address an even wider array of problems.

We could give endless advice on how to deal with difficult people, overcome bad habits, lose weight, save your marriage, raise teenagers without acquiring gray hair (not possible unless you really are a saint). Quite frankly, we haven't the time, acumen nor sustainable interest to research every person's problem and dispense wisdom on how to solve it.

When you create and apply your own solutions, you build badly needed "muscle" in the life skills part of your being.

We encourage you to be creative, to listen to yourself more, and to others a little (or lot) less. Using this system, you devise an approach that works for you. In all truth, you've already been doing that, but haven't taken enough notice of how you've done so. This system will help you focus on what has already worked for you, as you develop, even hone, what will continue to work for you.

All we're saying in this rule of thumb is not to rely so heavily on what everyone else is doing and advising. It's okay to notice what works for others, and it just might help to mimic them. However, it's more likely you will be successful when applying your own solution because, as we've already explained, you are the expert of your life.

It's a matter of trust. We tend not to trust ourselves, especially when it comes to solving our own problems. After all, aren't we the dummy that got ourselves into the fix in the first place? Why would we look to ourselves to get out of it? That almost seems to make no sense.

However, when you create and apply your own solutions, you build badly needed "muscle" in the life skills part of your being. If you borrow someone else's solution, you can never quite obtain the same kind of muscle tone.

Keeping with the hammer analogy, all that we want to do here is help you from having to use a cold pack on your heart and soul should you be tempted to use someone else's heavy duty hammer on your brad-shaped problem.

---

8. Solutions focusing is not solutions forcing.

So Breathe & Give Your Creative, Imaginative Capacities Time To Work.

Even if you come up with the perfect solution conceptually, it just might not work when you translate it from theory to practice. There are so many variables to consider, not only what works for you, but also how it affects others when you apply it in real time. You don't have to give up the first time something doesn't work. But, you do have to take notice that it didn't work, and adjust something for the next attempt.

This is a rule of thumb that gives you permission to tweak, and if in doubt, tweak again. When something works, keep doing it. When something doesn't, adjust it by doing something a little bit differently.

We're not advising extremism in this program. We're really talking about thinking of what is doable, and when taking the next step, keeping mental notes of where those steps lead you and how others are affected by it.

When a solution doesn't work, it is not a failure but a discovery!

Fred (not his real name), a student

I tried solutions focusing on a problem while at school, and it worked pretty well. I thought about using the Matrix for a bad habit, nail biting. I came up with a few easy solution steps. The first one I tried didn't work, so I went to another one. It didn't work, either. I got frustrated and stopped trying.

A couple months later, I went back to the first solution step because while it didn't work how I wanted at first, I still thought it was a good idea. The second time around, it worked, and it has stuck. It's a little weird because I still bite one nail. I don't know why, but I'm happy that at least nine of my nails look great!

What I learned was that the solution was right, but the timing wasn't. The solution isn't perfect, but was a start and the change felt good.

When I think of something else I can do for that last nail I still bite on when I'm worried about stuff, I'll let you know!

Some of us want to have everything carved in stone. We think of something and try it. It works! Wow. We want to do it again and again. Sometimes this is pure magic, a solution that works right out of the box, and keeps on working, every time we apply it.

Other times, when we use a solution for a second or third time, it doesn't work. Huh? We get anxious and mentally shout, "Hey, what's wrong with my solution?" Nothing. It's okay. Solutions are not absolutes.

They are simple techniques or strategies that may or may not work in the present moment when we apply them. Whether they work or not, they always supply useful information that helps us move toward what will work even better. That's all.

While problems may hurt, solutions don't have to. Be kind to yourself when working through a solution. Allow yourself mental and emotional room to make adjustments, all the while moving forward. Otherwise, you can get discouraged and then the old habit of wallowing around in the problem will return.

9. Complaining about others never creates solutions.

Don't Give Your Power Away. Be Your Own Boss!

Our problems are often deeply entwined with how others occupy our lives. In some cases, the person we are complaining about is hurting us. We want to be very clear. If that is the case, you need to reconsider that relationship altogether. Again, seek professional help (therapist, pastor, group support) in this regard.

Spending time and energy complaining about others diverts us from using that same very precious time and energy doing what we most need to be doing to rise above our problem.

Taking stock of yourself is not the same as being selfishly indulgent. Doing some honest self-assessment *minus* the judgment part takes you back to Socrates' golden rule: "Know thyself and to thine own self be true." In regard to golden rules, remember the universal one, and treat yourself as you want others to treat you.

More than you may have realized, you've ignored the healthy signs your body, mind and soul have been sending you for quite some time, informing you about the` consequences of things you've been doing, or the people you've been involved with.

Now, it's time to start listening to your higher self, the part of you that wants to heal, and re-engage others in new, more meaningful ways. When was the last time you laughed out loud for no other reason than you felt so good about your life in general? At least it's time to start seeing some good along with all the bad we so readily notice!

If Anne Frank could come to the conclusion that people are essentially good, in spite of having to hide in an attic, because those otherwise good people harbored dark and dangerous fears that would, and eventually did, threaten her life, we can surely come to a similar conclusion that there are better days ahead of us.

THE WHOLE TRUTH AND NOTHING BUT THE TRUTH IS THAT YOU CANNOT FIX ANYONE BUT YOURSELF.

In other words, Anne Frank came to her conclusion because she refused to dwell in complaint about others. She refused to give them *that* amount of control over her life. That did not mean they did not deserve such complaint. They deserved that and a lot more. However, she spent her time choosing her focus — on writing her diary and developing her own sense of hope for humanity.

How many millions have her words inspired since then? And those who thought they had destroyed her legacy by getting rid of her? They are all in the "forgotten" pile of human history.

We've all had to suffer under the occasional someone who has made us miserable, some temporarily so, and others for much longer periods of time, be it a bad boss, angry spouse, rebellious teenager, back-stabbing colleague or a friend whose choices in life impacted us in toxic ways. When creating a solution, one may keep such people in mind, but the solution is never in trying to fix them.

Listen up. You've heard this before, but if you just haven't been able to believe it, then we hope this reiteration of it somehow gets through. The whole truth and nothing but the truth is that you cannot fix anyone but yourself.

We don't mean that you ignore people who need your help, but in the end, the best help you give anyone else ends up being support for them while they work things out for themselves.

It could also happen that as you work on your solutions, and begin to heal old wounds, becoming more fully who you really are, others might respond to the reverberations of your effort. It's possible they might become inspired and address their issues in tandem with you.

That's a bonus, but it cannot be your primary focus and/or goal. Your goal is to pay better attention to yourself and formulate solution steps you know that you can do, and thus are more likely to do. Without a doubt, if you take such steps, others will experience an effect, but this is a bonus for you, as well as for them.

Solutions Rule #10 ... wait for it...!

Many of the SRTs you've just read have been distilled from a genre of academic and clinical study we've earlier introduced to you, known as Solution Focused Brief Therapy. But this rule of thumb comes straight from the essential core character of Karen's mind, heart, and soul.

If you happen to know the characters from Winnie the Pooh stories, Karen could be compared to Tigger, a youthful, energetic tiger, while Marilyn tends to be like Eeyore, the morose donkey. Of course, they each have opposite qualities as well, as most people are not completely optimistic nor pessimistic.

But, this Rule of Thumb is one that both authors play with, usually Karen being the one to remind Marilyn of SRT #10, to which Marilyn grumbles, but always gets on board and complies. Whichever character above you might resemble, we give you permission to use it anywhere, anytime.

We encourage and give you permission to at times enjoy all the changes you will be making for yourself. Some changes will be serious, true, but even serious efforts can be fun.

We don't mean you have to be slaphappy necessarily, though silliness has its place in all our lives. We mean that since you are rearranging the furniture in your personal and professional spaces, you might as well fling open a window and dance around in the fresh air time to time.

So, here is Karen's unique addition to the Solutions Rules of Thumb, her #10 (which she uses often enough to make it a #1 ... and if you need further explanation, then seriously, you really should read this book cover to cover).

10. Look for the FUN!

Look for the FUN! in your solutions, your relationships, your home, your work, your life …

Because, if you do, you will find it.

Guaranteed.

Part III: Setting Your Course Using The Matrix

5. The Solutions Matrix

Your solutions GPS.

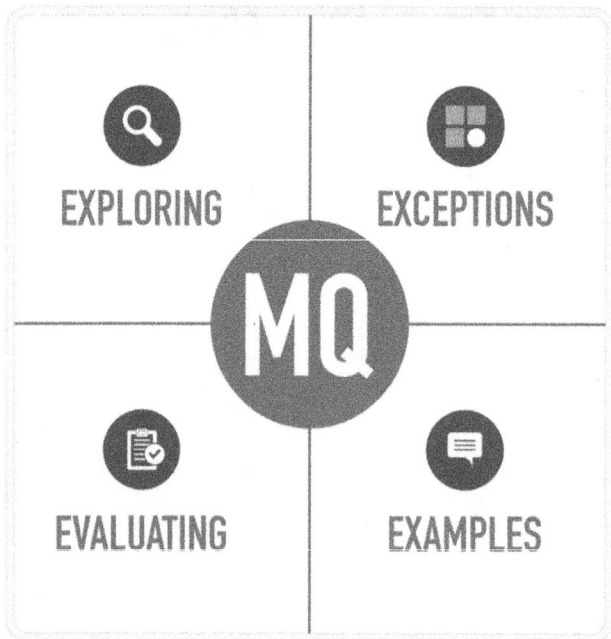

We are now getting you ready to set out to sea. Be aware your voyage is likely to encounter unknown winds and waves, currents and surprises. There are no visible roads out there, no dotted lines to follow, no tracks or milestones. Just context and choices. Having a compass makes an enormous difference when it comes to choosing a direction in which to move.

In this chapter, we are going to introduce you to the nuts and bolts of the Solutions Mastery System. In time, you will become adept with the entire System, which includes the Principles and Rules as well as the Matrix we are going to take you through in this section of the book.

The core component of the System is the Solutions Matrix, and at the heart of this Matrix is a question that has been used over decades with tens of thousands of clients in Solution Focused Brief Therapy. That question is simply called, the Miracle Question. In our Matrix, we refer to it as the MQ.

Surrounding that question in the Matrix are four lines of inquiry that guide you to imagine, design and implement solutions based upon you as the expert of your life. It is not a one and done proposition. Using the Matrix becomes a way of life, but not as you might think. It doesn't change your choice of religion, political point of view, social standing or whom you consider as family, friends and colleagues.

The Matrix may change your conversations and relationships with all of the above, and usually in very positive ways. We can assure you that it doesn't become an alternative or opposing way of life from the one you're already leading. On the other hand, it does become a new way to formulate your values and approach your relationships in a solution-focused rather than problem-oriented way.

Many of the changes you enact may be quite small, but nonetheless, effective. Sometimes, however, changes may occur on a much larger magnitude of scale than you could have ever foreseen.

Using the Matrix can be a bit like opening one of Forest Gump's boxes of chocolates. You never quite know what you are going to get, except that it will be different from what you've gotten before. This system opens you to examining areas of your inner world that you may have set aside for many years, and perhaps for good reason.

While things are going to change for you, let us reassure you that you remain in control of the decisions you make toward those changes. If you feel that some of the changes you've enacted are overwhelming, you can always scale it down. The Matrix simply allows you to try solutions on for size. It gives you a way to practice new thoughts, new feelings, and most importantly, new behaviors. You decide if the shoe fits and is worth wearing.

To some extent, you can adjust the intensity of change, up or down. If you take a jog with some upward and downward slopes, you discover that you need to adjust your breathing accordingly. As you go up a hill, you will naturally breathe slower and harder, but as you go down, your breathing gets quicker and easier. Using the Matrix is very similar. You adjust the speed of change, as well as the size of change to what you can handle, no more, no less.

There is a caveat that needs repeating. While you may be able to tweak your own speed and/or size of change, you cannot always predict how others will react to those same changes. Often when you are moving in a positive direction, others will notice and appreciate what you are doing, and they are likely to reciprocate with something positive as well.

However, humans are only somewhat predictable and this isn't always the case. Some people seem to like things to remain the way they are, even if those situations have been anything but happy. The old saying, "misery loves company" is a common expression for a reason.

For example, you may have a longtime friend with whom you often meet at lunch. Only now, after becoming familiar with solutions focusing, you no longer want to complain about work during that brief respite. You'd rather explore new approaches rather than continually rehash the same old problems.

Your friend might find the new conversation challenging, and their reaction can vary. They might delight in the fact that you don't complain as much and your friendship might deepen in new ways. On the other hand, they might wish you'd continue to wallow around in the muck with them and re-direct the conversation toward places you no longer want to go.

The Matrix has a component that will help you deal with such reactions in a non-defensive way. We discuss how to do this later in the chapter about Exploring.

While change can be unsettling, it can also be interesting and exciting. We keep encouraging you to embrace the change, because, after all, it's what you really want (or you wouldn't be here).

So, having touted it enough in this and previous chapters, let's get you started on how to use the Solutions Matrix as your own personal "Solutions Compass."

6. The Miracle Question

"Suppose that one night..."

EXPLORING

EXCEPTIONS

MQ

EVALUATING

EXAMPLES

Karen likes to describe the Matrix as a dexterous hand, with the Miracle Question acting like the thumb and the 4 lines of inquiry as the fingers. We've mentioned Solution Focused Brief Therapy (SFBT), and while the co-founders did not use a Matrix, per se, they did come up with several components of it, the key one being the Miracle Question (MQ).

The MQ, like many great discoveries, came about almost accidently. InSoo Berg (a foundational innovator of SFBT with Steve de Shazer, and his spouse) recounts how one of her clients found her problem so overwhelming that she wailed, "It would take a miracle to solve my problem!" InSoo immediately responded with, "Okay, let's say you got your miracle and your problem disappeared. What would you be doing differently from what you're doing now?"

The client was initially stumped, but slowly began to describe herself as having a fairly normal morning. She didn't imagine any huge changes, but simply painted a picture of an hour in her life without all the worry and stress that had brought her to the clinic in the first place.

InSoo's follow-up question was, "Do you think you could go home and function like that for an hour there?" The client thought about it, and then agreed that she could probably live in the way she described for at least an hour.

In later sessions, she was encouraged to extend that hour into a day, and that day into a week, and so on. The MQ genie was now out of the therapeutic bottle.

The client's exclamation and InSoo's response was something of an "aha" moment for SFBT. Since it worked for this client, they decided to "do more of that" and tried the question as a scenario for other clients.

Here is a version of the scenario they devised to help clients imagine, if only for a few minutes, what life might be like without the problem having center court in their lives:

Suppose that one night, while you were asleep, there was a miracle and this problem was solved. You were sleeping, so you were not even aware that this miracle had happened. What would be different? How would others know without your saying a word to them that your problem was solved? Imagine yourself in that morning. Watch yourself like a fly on the wall. What do you notice that you are doing differently? What evidence would you see/hear/sense that the miracle has happened and your problem is solved?

This is one of many variations of the MQ, and yes, if you noticed there is more than one question in the scenario, it still all boils down to one: *What would you be doing differently if you did not have that problem in your life?*

Take your time with this. We advise you set aside 10-15, even 20 minutes. We aren't used to sitting still and allowing our imagination to take over, but this is the most effective way to use the MQ.

Find a fairly comfortable chair, but not too comfortable. We don't want you to fall asleep mid-exercise. Sit up straight, but remain relaxed. We do want you to be alert.

Read the scenario out loud. It helps to hear the MQ question(s) as they prod you to think of life without the problem in it.

Allow yourself to freely imagine waking up and going about the first moments of your day in a wonderful state of peace that not having the problem would bring to you. For a few minutes, *live*, if only at first in your imagination, without the pressure, worry, burden, stress and other ill effects of your problem.

Further imagine that you are a fly on the wall and watch yourself wake up, stretch your arms in a relaxed manner and yawn as if you haven't a care in the world. Now, take your time and gently imagine what you would do as you get ready for work or whatever the day requires of you, but never let the problem enter into the picture. Only imagine your life without it.

This exercise does several things. First, it gives you some respite, if only emotionally (and this is no small thing), from the problem. Second, it allows you to envision what you want to do, rather than what you don't want to do. If your only focus is on what you don't want, all that is accomplished is a minus, not a plus.

By the way, we have to make a very important distinction here. Pay attention to the language because this is a somewhat subtle, but absolutely essential point. You cannot use a "not" when devising a solution. What do we mean by this?

When creating and building upon a solution, you can only use a positive, a thought or action that you want to have, or do, to effect a change. It's impossible to change anything from a "not to do."

For example, if you say, "I don't want to smoke anymore," all you've done is describe what you don't want to do, but you haven't described any kind of thought, feeling or behavior that you want to do differently from smoking.

When creating and building upon a solution, you can only use a positive, a thought or action that you want to have, or want to do, to effect a change.

You can imagine wearing a nicotine patch, or chewing some kind of gum, or other new, better habits. The one thing that will never help you find a solution, and likewise never help you wean away from this unhealthy addiction is to continually bemoan that you don't want to smoke!

Certainly, having the motivation to stop doing something is good, even necessary. But, simply stating what you don't want gets you not one step closer to changing the behavior itself. You have to decide what it is that you *do* want to do.

There's a little bonus here. Spending time with the MQ is a mini-vacation you can take anytime, anywhere, even on a subway train if you're really good at blocking out noise—just don't forget to get off at your station! It gives you a bit of respite from "all that." In the meantime, you might see something in your imagination that leads you to a solution step, so it's a win-win, always, for you.

And, of course, don't forget to have some fun, because in this exercise of imagining yourself free of the problem, you can *do* whatever you want. You might as well imagine doing interesting things that make you happy.

Solutions, after all, do not have to be commensurate with the problem. The problem might be deep and dark, but your solution could be just the opposite. It could be a lighthearted and humorous approach. Why not?

Don't discount what you imagine. You might not be able to exactly recreate your MQ moment in real life, but the point is to imagine living differently without the problem. It is not meant to be a flight from reality, however.

What you are looking for, in this exercise is what you do want to be doing in your life. You already know what you don't want – the problem, whatever it is.

The MQ allows you to look at your life differently. That's the key point. The MQ asks you to open your mind, heart and body to hope, to seeing, feeling, and experiencing your life without having to contend with the problem currently impeding it.

So, yes, yes, yes! You are allowed to hope, although we do understand that when you are deep down in the pit of a problem, hope seems like a luxury.

However, hope is not a luxury. Hope is essential to creating solutions. Think about it. If you are truly hopeless, then searching for solutions is a total waste of time.

When you review the Principles at Play and the Rules of Thumb, there is a great deal of material in those chapters that is hopeful. You might not be able to solve your problem in its entirety, but, to use just one of the SRTs, you can always make small changes within your sphere of influence, no matter what. And so, there's always a bit of hope.

Problem Experts focus on what they don't want, which is the problem, and don't spend enough time thinking about what they do want, which is the solution.

Consider someone who was reduced to a very small sphere of influence, a prison of only a few square yards.

The Terry Anderson Story

Terry Anderson, a hostage for 444 days in Iran following the turbulent overthrow of the Shah in the 1970s.

He described how his world shrank to the size of a dusty, squalid prison cell where he was chained to the middle of the floor. The guards worked hard to make him and his fellow hostages miserable. The psychological and physical torture was relentless on a daily, even hourly basis.

In the midst of this, he decided that the one thing they could not take from him was the freedom to choose. And so, he chose hope, even while knowing he could very well die without seeing his family again.

Every morning he chose to remain hopeful that someday he would see his family. This afforded him a strength he did not expect to have and he endured to the extent that one guard eventually expressed admiration toward him.

This is a fairly extreme example of being able to effect change within one's sphere of influence. Few of us will ever have to create a solution under the pressures of what a hostage must face. So, if hope can be generated in those circumstances, then surely we can have hope in the midst of the challenges confronting us.

For this reason, the MQ is a wonderful opportunity to open the windows of your mind and allow the soft breeze of hope to waft through. In fact, the more you do it, the more you not only find open windows, but doors as well. You won't have to get a ladder and crawl your way out of a problem. You'll just open the door and walk through it with a creative array of simple solutions that you have devised for yourself.

A Step-by-Step Guide Through The Miracle Question:

1) Write The Question Down: Find a sheet of paper. Write down the MQ scenario as described at the beginning of the chapter. It's only a paragraph, but writing and then reading it quietly out loud to yourself helps you place the question in your mind and body.

2) Give Yourself A Little Time to Imagine: Make sure you've given yourself enough time to ease into and remain with this question. It's important to sit with it, to allow it to rise in your mind. Read the MQ scenario, then close your eyes and imagine yourself, step by step, waking up and going through the first few moments of your day free of the worries and stress of that problem.

3) Notice: It's important to notice what you do, and not so much what you might be thinking or feeling. Doing is essential in any solution you create, so imagining what you will do while free of your problem helps you in the next step of the exercise.

4) Feel it: After clarifying what you will be doing, then lean into how that feels. After you've spent some time enjoying life *without* your problem (doesn't it feel good?), jot down a few notes about the things you noticed yourself being able to do in that problem-free space.

Keep noticing your actions, and when you notice yourself thinking something you haven't thought before, jot those new thoughts down as well.

If you can only imagine your life without the problem for 5-10 minute intervals, that's all you need to get started. Each time you use this question, stay a little longer in your problem free life! Hey, why not?

Eventually, you'll be able to imagine an hour without that problem, and then a morning. After a few runs of this exercise, you can imagine an entire day where the problem does not present itself.

In your imagination, time is very relative. You can envision an hour, or an entire day equally in the space of about 20 minutes. You will be amazed how much you can imagine getting done in a problem free day. Likewise, you'll be surprised how much you get done in real life when you are solutions, not problem, focused.

To summarize, what the MQ allows us to do, in a very direct manner, is look at how we really want to live, if only we could. Nothing stops any one of us from living how we truly want in our imagination.

It's just that simple, though not always that easy. Sometimes it is that easy and we come up with the perfect little solution step right away. Other times, it takes a little bit of mental muscle and we have to visit the MQ exercise a few times to figure out just what it is we want to do next.

But, hard work can be fun. If you've given yourself wholeheartedly to an endeavor, such as tending your garden, writing a poem, playing a good game of tennis, practicing a dance, or whatever activity brings you joy, you know the satisfaction of exerting yourself toward a desired end.

The MQ is a way, and a core one at that, to investigate what your life will be like without a particular problem. In effect, it's a way to imagine what you will do, what steps you are prepared to take, in a solution-oriented, not problem-centered, format.

Imagine, imagine, imagine. Notice, notice, notice. Jot down, jot down, jot down. Then, do, do, do. One little step at a time, then bigger steps, and so forth. You get the idea.

The trick is to keep it real, even though it's an exercise of the imagination. Don't fly off to a remote island, unless you can really do that, and it somehow is a positive step that solves your problem.

The purpose of this exercise, along with the other parts of the Matrix is to help you figure out what you really want to do, what small, doable steps you are willing to take in order to make those small changes within your sphere of influence.

Who am I & what Do I really want?

As you recall, over time, those small shifts accumulate and become bigger changes. Eventually, it will become fun, maybe not at the beginning, but surely over time, we promise you will find the fun in your changes!

We've experienced it for ourselves all too often, and have had the happy headache of hearing the same report, repeatedly, from fellow Matrix practitioners.

Albert Einstein once defined insanity as doing the same thing you've done before while expecting different results. The MQ is one way to stop the insanity of having the same conversation about your problems and somehow expecting changes to happen.

By imagining yourself doing something different, and then doing that different thing in real life, you can most certainly expect different results. In the next few chapters, we will look at four other ways to further enhance the sanity inducing impact of using the Solutions Matrix regularly in your life.

The MQ may be the least specific of the Matrix, in the purpose of creating actual solution steps. It's greatest service to all who use it is to get your mind into a solutions focusing mode, to turn your thoughts from all about the problem to life without the problem.

It can be compared to the broad strokes needed on a canvas to create background and depth. The MQ allows you to see life without the problem in it, to notice things you would be doing instead.

The lines of inquiry described in the next four chapters are more like the detail of the painting, the exact strokes, the little changes, and doable steps that you envision and do in order to live within your solution, not your problem.

7. The Exceptions Line of Inquiry

When did things go right?

EXCEPTIONS

As you start to practice the Matrix, you will soon discover that you don't use all 5 lines of inquiry at the same time. Nor do you need to use them in the order we present. The MQ is the core question, and you may tend to use it more often at first. Some do not as they are so entangled with the problem they can't even let themselves imagine their life without it. Eventually however, you will find that you prefer one line of inquiry over another and the chances are this preference will change over time.

We start with Exceptions because it is a very simple way to stimulate and experience turning from what feels normal, that is, dwelling on problems. The Exceptions Line of Inquiry begins your journey as a detective (or perhaps researcher) into areas of your life where the kernels of solutions have been hiding.

Noticing when a problem was not happening, or in other words, noticing *when things went right*, is a way of peeping through the door and seeing where the pink elephant in the room is *not* located.

While people often avoid talking about the proverbial pink thing in the room, that doesn't mean they aren't preoccupied with it. Quite the opposite. Were they not oppressed by or strangely fascinated with this hulk in their midst, they would more freely talk about it, indicating that the thing (problem) doesn't really weigh so much upon them.

Learning to notice what goes right takes just that, a little learning. Because the emotions that problems evoke are so consuming, it is little wonder they significantly shape the way we see the world. So when problems are all consuming, a little intervention is a good thing!

What is really fun about exceptions is that even when exceptions are accidental, what we can glean from them is as valuable as known-to-be-successful experience.

So knowing that problems simply are not the whole truth of our lives, when we "do a JS2" to look for those exceptions to our problem, then we have jumpstarted our solutions building.

Go on, take 2 minutes right now, and with just one specific problem in mind, look for one or two (or more) exceptions, those times when your problem wasn't happening.

Now, when you probe further into those gaps, and think about the situation from the "what went right (even if only a few things, or just one thing) perspective," the elements of solutions begin to surface. These exceptions to the problem also help us remember that there really are ways to live without the problem while providing us with real-life examples of what *to* do.

Take for example a young woman who feels terrible about a broken relationship. It is the second one in a row for her, and she is seeking how to engage others in her life in ways that do not lead to this same result.

This line of inquiry may well be a great starting point for her as she is a smart, successful person who accomplishes much professionally, but just tends to be self-critical and feels as if she is a failure in her personal world. And this kind of harsh judgment of the good and easy exaggeration of the bad is well, pretty human.

Studies have shown that humans adjudge the impact of the good and the bad rather unevenly. This was demonstrated in a study in which nm m, subjects were presented with the following.

From a Study

A corporate executive is faced with a decision to promote a product that would considerably improve his company's bottom line, but would have an adverse environmental impact.

On the other hand, he could choose to shelve the product until a later time when it could be produced without such effect, thus sparing the environment, but costing his company substantial sums of money.

In the first scenario, the executive moves ahead with the product. In the second one, he declines to do so. The scores tell it all. For doing the "good thing," the exec was given an approval rating of 38%. For doing the "bad" thing, he was given a disapproval rating of 72%.

*We lost track of this exact study. However the point about negativity bias and negativity dominance remain. You can find many more studies on this issue, some of them listed in the resources section.

Numbers don't lie. We look at things we've done, giving the bad much more weight than it probably deserves while making light of the real good we've managed to do in our lives, and sometimes in spite of solid odds against us doing it!

Sometimes, when we've made a mistake, we have to stop from giving ourselves the usual whack on the forehead. Instead, we need to pause and recall the good that we did, then give ourselves a little pat on the shoulder.

So back to our young lady and her "unsuccessful" relationship. It would help her to recognize that not everything about her previous relationship was bad.

Looking for exceptions asks her to look for those times in the relationship when the problem between them was *not* happening.

The point of the exercise is not to convince her that she should re-invest in the relationship, although that could happen. Rather, it is for her to focus on the things that *did* go right in that relationship, the ones she is currently choosing to overlook. By choosing to see what worked alongside what didn't, she is effectively giving herself new ways to think *and* feel about herself.

If all she does is look back and feel miserable about all that went wrong, filtering out all that did go right, she is limiting herself to a set of negatively framed options: 1) deciding not to enter into a new relationship because it will probably fail; 2) being almost 100% bound to bring all those feelings of failure *into* any next relationship, making every relationship harder to succeed from the get go; or 3) going back into that relationship and most likely messing up again because she has not yet figured out what works! It's a perfect recipe for failure every which way.

By unearthing those times when the problem was *not* happening, she has opened a window to thoughts and ideas not constrained to doom and gloom scenarios. Now what is needed are a few more specifics about how to recreate similar circumstances in the future. That's where the next line of inquiry into Examples comes in.

In short, Exceptions are the skeleton keys helping us unlock the possibility of solutions and the reality is that each of us has those keys in our lives already! But we do have to look for them, and that, no one else can do for us. Others can help guide us to that trough of water, even urge, encourage, support us. But like that proverbial horse, we are the ones who have to take in those cool waters. We are the only ones who can sift and sort through our past to find what *did* work for us and to be soothed and encouraged by that knowledge!

Looking back at when the problem was not happening not only helps us see what we and others were doing right, it also helps us look at the present and future in a more positive, less problem oriented way.

We begin to see little things going right even in the midst of a sticky problem as it unfolds. This helps us get through the daily stuff of life in a much more fluid manner. We don't get as easily bogged down with what's going wrong, but instead, keep ourselves and others buoyed by what we notice is going right.

Gradually, as you focus on what's going right, and encourage more of whatever that is to happen in yourself and others, your thinking becomes less heavy with gloom and doom Problem Expert storm clouds hanging overhead. You do begin to think, feel and live in a lighter and brighter way. And your better moments become even better yet!

You might say this a pie in the sky promise. It might be. However, it is our personal experience that it really is more fun to focus on what's going right in one's life. Of course, you can keep digging down into your deep pit of problems, and stay there, wallowing away.

We won't stop you. In fact, we can't stop you. Only you can stop you from doing that. We have come to the conclusion and consider the Problem Expert way of life as somewhat insane. We look back at the years we lived like that and wonder how we ever got through it all without losing our minds.

The point is, we nearly did lose our minds, and hearts, and almost our very souls. Hopefully, though, we've at least convinced you to try doing some things differently in your life. But, if Einstein could not convince you as to the difference between sane and insane, (doing the same thing over and over while expecting different results), then we don't have the hubris to think we could, either.

8. The Examples Line of Inquiry

How did I do that?

EXAMPLES

So now we get to the part that gives us the practical tools for solutions construction. Remember, even if that exception was totally accidental, it still holds the keys to solutions for you!

Now with that exception to the problem in mind, it's time to get specific about what we (and others) were doing. It's time to notice who/what/where/when things were going right, when the problem was not happening. What we can identify then become the resources we can turn to, to recreate exceptions to the problem!

Now it's time to linger a little longer (OK, only 2 minutes) with those exceptions. The focus here is on the specific behaviors, words, perspectives, people, choices, locations, thoughts and encounters—all those things that left little to no room for the problem.

We all have good and bad behaviors. The difference between success and failure resides in becoming more conscious and consistent about identifying and using our "good stuff."

So how do we identify and use our good stuff? Sometimes it's as simple as…PLAYing, you know the little 4-part system we introduced earlier (and will mention again later)? Here are the steps again:

1) Pausing to remember we do have a choice in how we deal with our problem, now that we have identified at least one exception;

2) Lean into the moment and take this time as you breathe to focus on one exception, recalling some of the examples the who/what/where/words/feelings when that exception was happening;

3) Adapt those examples to your present situation, envisioning how you might use what you know has worked before, as you now deal with this similar problem;

4) EnjoY and celebrate this unveiling of a new way forward you have just set out for yourself!

What you glean from these 2 minutes will provide a new track to run when your problem comes a-knocking. This you didn't have before!

Bev (not her real name), a student

I have long suffered with excess weight connected to stress-related eating and likewise, stress-related lack of exercise. A few years ago, the weight had caused enough health issues that my doctor ordered a stress test. Fortunately, things indicated that I was borderline "okay," but I still needed to lower the blood pressure and cholesterol numbers.

That motivated me because I did not want to take pills the rest of my life. I had to reflect on days when I did not overeat, and begin to copy the good behavior from those days into my present life. In my reflection, I recalled how much I enjoy salads. I decided that, since I have to eat out a lot in the line of work that I do, I would choose restaurants where I knew they made really good salads and that would be my main course. I didn't have to look high and low. A lot of restaurants these days, even some fast food establishments, cater to my kind of customer.

It's a process. I didn't adopt a macro-biotic diet. However, I've greatly improved from wolfing down hamburgers and fries, to the point where my diet is mostly plant based. Along with fresh salads and lightly steamed vegetables, I've come to enjoy frothy green drinks.

Remarkably, over the past few years, I've lost nearly 30 pounds. What else did I discover when I reflected back and noticed when things were going right? I recalled how I loved to swim, so I joined a gym and started swimming again. I also bought a mountain bike on sale at a great price, fixed a comfy seat on it and now take several rides a week, usually in the evenings. An unexpected bonus is that I've come to know a few more neighbors this way, and that has added some interesting people to my life.

Some weeks I'm better at both ends, diet and exercise. Some weeks, I slip into the old ways, but the slippage is less and doesn't last very long. I cannot recall, for example, when I've last had a fast food burger with a side of fries. I no longer even have the desire for that kind of "un-happy" meal.

Again, solutions focusing is not solutions forcing. It is a process, and usually a rather gentle one. Positive recall is looking back to reflect upon good things that you've accomplished, rather than all the mistakes you've made. This isn't being dishonest. It's being honest about yourself in a more useful way.

In fact, if you look back and *only* find mistakes, then you are lying to yourself. Yep. You are *lying*! Remember, everyone is doing the best they can, in their given context (beliefs, feelings, actions, relationships).

If all you do is think (assumptions) that you cannot change, then you won't have much desire (feelings) to change, so it follows that you won't change (actions) all that much, and you will be stuck with living your life in a way you don't want to be living (relationships).

However, if you do believe you can change, might you at least try something a little different, say, read a self-help book about change?! If so, you might be persuaded by the co-authors to change your assumptions and consider that at least small changes are possible.

If so, you will make those small changes, and move forward. Sure, you may revert to old bad habits, but then, you'll take that in as information and make some more small changes, and keep moving forward.

It isn't that you suddenly become a whole new person. That can happen in some religions, but even there, the word "backsliding" occurs in many a sermon for a reason.

In solutions building, we don't worry so much about backsliding. Such relapses are an inconvenient truth, that we are always a work in progress. Even so, they provide us with useful information. We cover a few more points about backsliding in a later chapter.

Solutions focusing is a practice, something we do on a daily basis. Some days we get closer to our goal, whatever it is and for whatever purpose we've designed it. Some days we have less energy, or other persons involved in the problem have more influence upon our behavior, and we slip slide around, reverting, reversing, revisiting old haunts and habits, etc.

The goals can change, and often do as we use different parts of the Matrix. When we bring good things we've done in our past forward into our present, a pattern tends to emerge. We find that we tend to slip into those unwanted behaviors less often, and when we do slip, we get out of that behavior more quickly than we did before.

Why? We have learned to stop focusing on the slippage, which is the problem. Okay, it happens, get over it. This leaves us time and energy to look back to another day when we used one of our solution steps. We recall that it worked rather well. Why not use it again today, or tweak it and see if that solution is even more helpful?

This leads us to the next line of inquiry, "Evaluating," where we use very simple math (can you count to ten?) to measure the days we experience the problem less problematically.

Using this line of inquiry over a period of time gives us, literally, a graphic picture of days when we did better than other days. And yes, you've got it by now. We then reflect on strategies we used on those days when we kept the problem at bay, and whatever it was that we were doing, we do more of that.

9. Evaluating

What's the difference?

EVALUATING

The essential question we ask, when using this Line of Inquiry is, "What was the difference?" By asking this question we are hoping to notice more about the nature of the difference *and* what made the difference.

The idea is simply to scale the impact of the problem(s) on days past and now. The lower numbers represent days when the problem was more present, and higher numbers when things were less difficult.

Most Matrix users report that they start with the Miracle Question, then look into Exceptions which leads them to think of Examples and from there, they devise action steps.

Many tend to skip over the Evaluating line of inquiry and get on with Exploring, i.e., gathering information from others' reactions to the solutions they employ. However, there are some who find this line of inquiry very helpful alongside each of the other lines of inquiry. A few approach it as the first part of their solutions creating program.

Marilyn

I don't know why, but when I first started using the Matrix, I found the MQ far too intimidating. I latched on instead to the Evaluating Line of Inquiry. I was in such a state of despair that I could not use the scale with positive numbers. It seemed like such a simple thing to look into my recent past and scale the days 1-10. However, I didn't have a lot of positive things going for me and I couldn't even resonate with "positive" numbers.

So, I measured my days from -10 to -1. A zero day would indicate that at least nothing bad had occurred. What happened next was interesting.

Gradually, as I reflected over recent events, I was able to see a pattern of "not so awful" days emerging. When I reflected on why those days were better, I couldn't think of anything at all. However, I was encouraged that some days were indeed better than others.

I asked, "What was the difference?" and no definitive answers came to mind. But, I was intrigued and wanted to find out why some days were better than others, so I began to use the Exception and Example lines of inquiry. I discovered something so simple that it should have been obvious all along, but I guess that's the reason why the Matrix is useful. People don't see the obvious a lot of the time.

The "not so bad" days were days after I had had a good night's sleep. I have trouble sleeping, but I did more work on the Examples inquiry and realized that when I went to bed just one hour earlier, I slept better. I'm still working on my problems, oops, I mean solutions, but this discovery, starting with the Evaluating Line of Inquiry has been a big help.

This line of inquiry tends to require some lineal space. By that, we mean, generally you can't scale for just one day and get an accurate reading of your situation. You need to take stock from day to day, over a period of time.

There may or may not be a pattern that stands out, but if one does stand out, pay close attention to it. Are your good days only on Saturday? Mondays? Thursdays? If so, what are you doing differently on those good days? How might you bring the good things you are doing on the higher numbered days into the lower numbered days?

We usually go to Exceptions when gleaning information from the recent past, the last few weeks or so, rather than use it to assess between distant comparative memories.

You will come to your own conclusions when using this scaling system because what you do differently from day to day is what you do, and how you want to use that information is how you want to use it.

The Evaluating scales help us discover good days from bad days, and then, to reflect on what is different about those good days. That's when we reach for Examples and follow that Line of Inquiry.

If we're stumped, we pull back on the throttle and perhaps float above a good day, in the mode of the MQ and recall how we lived relatively free of the problem that given day.

As we begin to more effectively use our lines of inquiry, we start to cause ripple effects in all areas of our lives – you know, where those other people are, at home, the office, online and wherever else we come and go—our family, friends, colleagues, bosses, subordinates and those folks in line at the grocery store who are friendlier than we'd like them to be and start a conversation we don't exactly want to have, but sometimes end up enjoying anyway.

This leads us to the next Line of Inquiry, which is appropriately titled, "Exploring."

10. The Exploring Line of Inquiry

Say again?

EXPLORING

The Exploring Line of Inquiry is about noticing how others react to what we say and do, by *objectively* listening to what they say and do about what we've said and done. And yes, it is a circuitous process.

It's also about daring to be spontaneous and even unpredictable... and seeing what happens then. The whole idea behind exploring is to treat, at least in part, what happens in your life as part of a test. Not the test where you get graded (sorry to conjure that idea). But rather in the Groundhog Day kind of way where what you did is now providing you with information that is essential for improvement: feedback.

This feedback is always happening, but often we tend to ignore it, feel judged by it, think it has little to do with us, or realize it most certainly has something to do with us, but prefer not to deal with it. This line of inquiry requires a bit more introspection and "social muscle" than the other Matrix questions that lead to solution steps.

Again, while we can't drink at the trough for you, we can give you a few pointers that make this line of inquiry more obviously helpful, and even fun. It takes some getting used to, because we do tend to react when others are in essence critiquing us. Frankly, criticism is something that is going to happen one way or another, directly or indirectly, and what we are doing here is encouraging you to make it work *for* you.

Now it's rather obvious that we chose the word "Exploring" at least in part because it happened to be another nice "E" word. But more importantly, we chose it because we want you to try out an attitudinal stance that may be different to the one you habitually take in the midst of dealing with your problems.

We want to emphasize that you take a more playful, experimental, "try it and see" open attitude. A hopeful one if you like. Challenges often get our stomachs churning. But so does excitement. Can you find it in you to interpret the tumult in the pit of your stomach as the excitement that comes with of being on the verge of new discoveries? Because you are!

Now you have a chance to see feedback as good information, information that you can use differently than when the problem was settling in. When we accept the feedback coming to us, in whatever form, as information and only that and not as some kind of final judgment from anyone, we can be less defensive. Our stance becomes less reactive and it allows us to "see" and "hear" things differently.

Why take this seemingly stoic approach? (Don't worry, it isn't a really a stiff upper lip response, it just looks that way). Simply put, feedback is useful information—no, essential information. A non-defensive, non-reactive stance helps us maintain a clear mind with less emotional clutter so we can efficiently and effectively sort through that information and benefit from it!

This is a different kind of gift we want you to give yourselves at the end of a hard day at work. Or first thing in the morning, whenever that feedback comes at you! Further, as we've hinted, a non-defensive and non-reactive response often allows conversations—the ones with others and the ones in your own head—to open up in unexpected ways.

This can become quite an exciting line of inquiry and one you cannot do alone, unlike the others where self-reflection is the key component. In this line of inquiry, you begin to pay attention to how others react to what you say and do, but not in the same way you may have done up to now.

We all tend to worry when others make comments about things we've said and done. We are constantly getting such feedback and much of it can be useful if we let it become so. The trick is how to mentally and emotionally guide what others tell us about ourselves toward useful information.

When someone more or less critiques us, we usually feel something in our guts. One feeling is fear, "Uh, oh, they're judging me." And the other is anger, "What right do they have to judge me?!"

These responses are commonly known as a flight or fight. We can flee others' comments to us by ignoring and deflecting them, or by resisting and arguing against them.

Sometimes, we're lucky and someone gives us helpful insight about what we're doing, and they do so without judgment or condemnation. Sometimes, we're not so fortunate and get a blast of criticism form someone who is a real Problem Expert and their feedback feels like an attack (because it is!).

It is difficult to receive the latter kinds of remarks in any positive way. At least one thing that such feedback informs you of is that you might be working with, or living with, people who are emotionally unhealthy. And then, what you want to explore with that conclusion is who you really are, and what you really want, in regard to such people in your life.

This next example shows how one person addressed this issue of constant negative feedback. We realize it is similar to an earlier example where a fellow named Joe dealt with a bad boss.

We don't mean to go after bosses in this book. There are many good, even great bosses out there. We know. We've had them. And, we've both been in management positions for parts of our career paths (we tried to be, and certainly hope we were one of those good ones).

What we want to illustrate here, in choosing these two examples from practitioners of the Matrix, is that there are many solutions even to one or similar problems.

Beth (not her real name), a student

Years ago, Beth had a boss who was an overall pessimistic person. He was soft spoken and seemingly well-intentioned, but he had a way of putting things, at least when talking with her, that focused heavily on the negative aspect of whatever she said or did, even though he would give her relatively high performance scores.

She became increasingly anxious about his criticism, and as time went on, less objective about it. She began to see herself as he did, from a negative, problem oriented point of view. The good things that she accomplished seemed trivial, while the small mistakes she made from time to time were enlarged and took on a central role in her mind.

What was once a joy, her professional work, became a dreaded chore. The days seemed to go on forever and she was drained of all energy by the time she got home. It took longer, not just hours, but sometimes days, to recuperate from meetings with him.

Eventually, she sought out a therapist to help her deal with her anxiety over this negative relationship. After several months of therapy, which was helpful, she began to use the Matrix with permission from her therapist. When she got to the Exploring line of inquiry, things began to change. She began to take his criticism as information, nothing more, nothing less.

She decided that she needed to look for employment with a more emotionally healthy group of people, especially under a more positive kind of leadership.

It took several more months, but she eventually found another place of employment. When asked in the interview why she was leaving her previous employ, she had practiced the Matrix enough to authentically state who she was and what she really wanted.

The more she was able to emotionally detach from his words, the more she could more accurately evaluate them. Eventually, she realized that the constant negative phrasing of things had eroded her self-confidence. She realized that while some of the things he noticed about her was helpful information, a great deal was not.

Beth shared her honest assessment without naming names. She let them know her former boss was highly problem focused and would rarely notice the good things that his subordinates accomplished. She then said, "It's simple. I prefer to work with positive people and your online reviews showed me that most of your employees feel great about working here."

To Beth's pleasant surprise, she was hired and assigned to a supervisor known to laugh out loud at her own jokes, for good reason, as her jokes are usually quite humorous. More importantly, her supervisor believes in giving affirmation when good things are accomplished, and only occasionally will critique something that has gone wrong, as an opportunity to educate, not as a means of bringing someone down.

Beth has been employed with this company for a few years now and hopes to retire there.

When we get any kind of feedback, delaying our reaction is very helpful. The best way that many Matrix users have found is to simply take a long, slow breath. And then, smile, just a little, but not facetiously. And then, give yourself some time.

Thank the giver of the feedback, but don't commit to the critique, either by agreeing that it's all true, or denying it and saying they're all wrong. Let them know you appreciate their thoughts and that you will need a bit of time to think about it, and that you'll get back to them about it, if needed (and then do so in a timely manner).

It might be something you can respond to in less than an hour. It might be a very dense critique that will take a few days or even weeks to digest. This is for you alone to measure. The essential thing is that you give yourself the time you need to sit down in a safe space and further explore the information you've been given.

It's as good as any excuse for some "me time." Sit with one or more lines of inquiry and see what kinds of solutions their comments might lead you to discover.

Sometimes, when we're given positive feedback, we brush it off with a demur of some kind. We'd like to politely ask you to please stop doing that, at least sometimes, and check what it is you are reacting to.

We're not advocating you become a self-absorbed, attention seeking, egomaniac. But honestly, when people compliment you, take it for the positive feedback that it most likely is, unless you've somehow discerned they have a sycophantic need to falsely overestimate you. But even then, take it all in with a gracious and simple, "Thank you."

Don't qualify compliments! Don't respond with, "It wasn't all that much," or "Well, it was mostly luck."

Feedback is good information. If you receive a compliment, by all means, do more of that behavior. On the other hand, if you receive a complaint, by all means, sift through it with a solutions focus in mind. Remember that we weigh in with complaints more heavily than we do with compliments (72% versus 38%).

It is also an opportunity to assess what kind of person is giving you negative feedback. Is it just this one time? Or, do they always have something negative to say about you? If you are encountering constant negative feedback from someone, you might want to consider a few things.

Are they someone you need to keep engaging with? If so, what small changes can you make within your sphere of influence that might make this relationship less negative? Are they someone you can manage to spend less time with, or break entirely free from? If so, evaluate the pros and cons of associating with them.

Finding happy, healthy people to live and work with is a lifelong endeavor. In fact, becoming a happy, healthy person is the most effective way to ensure that such people become a part of your life. You know, "birds of a feather." Well, it is a rather true aphorism.

Using the Matrix on a regular basis is a remarkably easy way to take real steps toward that very worthy lifelong pursuit of overall happiness (which hopefully the Constitution will protect for some time to come).

Summary of the Solutions Matrix' Lines of Inquiry

So there you go. We have now looked at each line of inquiry. Once you have your new Solutions System in place you can expect to have the following:

- A shift in focus
- Knowledge of the underlying Principles and Rules of Thumb that are key to solutions implementation
- A copy of the Matrix in your pocket (you can print one from the resource section).

And then you are as good as halfway there, to wherever it is that you really want to be.

CONGRATULATIONS!

But wait! There's more!

Part IV:
You're On Your Way!

Whether you have realized it or not, you have already left the dock. If you were to look back for a moment, you would notice that the dock, your old way of looking at things, is already "way back there."

Sure you will want to come back to shore, but when you do, you will already *be* different. And all that is good.

So let's take a moment to look at a few extra things that just might be of use to you on your solution focused rather than problem oriented, forward looking rather than backward mulling, exciting (not to mention fun!) new journey in life.

11. Take Your BFF With You

Making Self-Talk Your Best Friend—Forever!
Overcome Silent Sabotage

Show me someone who doesn't have constant chatter going on in his or her head and you'll be showing me a dead person. We think, all the time. We think silently to ourselves and we think out loud in conversation. Some of us do both at the same time, engaging in a self-conversation out loud, usually in the shower where we hope no one else can listen in.

The brain is always assessing and giving us feedback, all day long and even in our sleep at night. Our head never stops in that regard.

Further and germane to this chapter, our thoughts seem so "true" to us that we believe them, for no other reason than we have thought them. This unquestioned believing of what we think, just because we think it, is one of the more irrational things we humans do.

We address this issue here because, just as when we assess others' behaviors, our self-assessment tends toward that 72% negative area, sometimes to the point where we convince ourselves that the problem is overwhelming – there is nothing we can do, and even if we tried, we lack the smarts, will power, resources, or support to make any significant change.

Believing our thoughts is akin to taking ourselves too seriously. We're not saying you should disbelieve every thought you think. That would be enticing you to cynicism. We are, however, encouraging you to at least question what you think, especially when your thoughts are critical and harsh.

These days, we hear about bullying in the schools and on social media. We all decry its negative impact, and some of us recall times when we stood up to a bully because he or she was putting down a friend or family member. We know that bullying is just as harmful in the form of verbal abuse as it is when delivered physically.

And yet, we will deliver to ourselves, blow by verbal blow, negative words about ourselves, that we're stupid, or ugly, or clumsy, or too shy, or not worthy of others' positive regard for us, and so on.

Some of us use a subtler, but nonetheless, detracting self-talk. We don't realize that when we think of others as being so very much better than we are in whatever category of comparison we choose, that we have inferred the opposite. We are in effect automatically making ourselves a lesser version of those we inordinately admire.

It isn't that we should never admire others, especially when they have done things of great value, and we aspire to do or be something similar in our own way. It is when we compare ourselves with phrases like, "I could never be or do that," and ignore our own good contributions to the human experience that we've crossed a line.

There is a difference between self-reflection and self-recrimination. Solutions Mastery is all about self-reflection, guiding you to think more clearly about who you really are and what you want, with regard to others (a la the Matrix).

You are not looking back to ruminate over the problem, but rather looking back and realizing you've done some good things after all.

This is **positive recall**, seeking out those moments when good things were happening, and reflecting on what you and others were doing, and then finding ways to replicate those good actions, going forward into the present and future.

Consider this: Would you allow another person to talk to you the way you talk to yourself when you're giving yourself a tongue-lashing for something that went wrong? What if one of your colleagues at work messed up a project and the boss came to their desk and yelled at them, calling them a lousy so-and-so? Would you feel their words were helpful to your colleague?

We've all experienced that, someone addressing us about something we've done in a way that is not in the least bit helpful to us. They don't spend the time to think about ways to instruct us as to how we might do better next time, or assist us to discover our own insights on how we might improve.

Marilyn

Honestly, don't you rather resent such persons? I know I did. Before I started using the Matrix, I used to battle with them. It only made them worse as they then sought every opportunity to make sure I understood just how right they were.

One thing the Matrix helped me realize and works for me is that I now spend as much time as I can with people who affirm me and accept my affirmation of them in return. The inverse of that means I spend as little time, if at all, with people who are mostly negative and only seem to find ways to criticize me and others in their rather dreary life.

We need to take what we say to ourselves in the same way the Matrix teaches us to accept feedback from others. Be polite to your thoughts, but let them know you'll take them into consideration and get back to them at a convenient time for you.

What we won't tolerate from others, we almost nonchalantly accept from ourselves. Or worse, we adamantly accept those thoughts, and disregard what others might have to say in a more positive light, as if their observations could simply never be as accurate as our own.

Here's the odd thing. Because we're the ones talking down to ourselves, we accept such negative thoughts as some kind of gospel truth. They aren't. Quite often the person least accurate in our assessment of ourselves is, ta da, ourselves.

Karen

Let me add a quick note here about our self-talk in light of our being the experts of our lives. There is no doubt that no one else knows as well as you do the ins and outs of your life, your priorities, aspirations, sense of mission (or not), what touch or twist or sound is most meaningful. So when we say, "You are the expert of your life," we mean it.

What is does *not* mean however, is that you always have the most accurate data on which to base your life decisions. While you, and only you are clearly best positioned to meaningfully utilize all the information, advice, ideas, and feedback that come to you, there is almost always room for improving the quality of what we decide to take seriously from others and ourselves.

While we more easily notice and assess external information by considering the source, timing and other factors, we are less discriminating regarding our own self-talk.

That is why I encourage you to reflect on how you speak to yourself. Do you speak to yourself appreciatively or derisively? I urge you to notice your internal commentary and adjust it. That you have complete control over! But in the end, whether the commentary is "nice" or "not nice" is less important than "Is it true?" You deserve good information upon which to make each decision in your life, especially from yourself.

This ties in with the emerging evidence that unconscious processing exerts influences on motivations, judgments, and behaviors. The impact of this "illusion-of-truth effect" is important to consider because our beliefs about ourselves form the basis for our behaviors.

So may I ask you to do one thing? The next time you start getting down on yourself, check the words and phrases you are using. Check if they are responsive or reactionary and most importantly, if they reflect the truth of the situation.

Let me be blunt for moment here: Don't lie to yourself. Don't demonize or adulate. Just speak as close to the truth as you can. I promise you, this small change will accumulate significantly!

In addition to the reactionary and very often untrue self-talk we engage in, we want you to notice when you find yourself actively seeking sympathy. While this is built-in from infancy, it is not always the most helpful way to get a solution. In fact, much of the time, sympathy seeking is an obstacle to solutions!

Breaking away from both–negative self-talk, and sympathy-seeking wallowing–can be easier than it might seem at first. True, it's practically an ingrained habit. But all that we're learning now is how to negotiate those same needs in our now adult voice.

A baby really does want warm milk and a dry diaper. Their only language is "Wah!" We might have a more sophisticated grasp of grammar, and our needs are more complex, but just as we don't think a baby is undignified to holler, "Wah!" why should we withhold from saying who we are and what we want with authentic words?

What is it anyway, in a nutshell, without all the "stuff" of life that we think we are and want?

We suggest, in one form or another, it boils down to rather simple, but essential two things: to love and be loved. In other words, we all want to be in happy, healthy relationships.

Many studies have shown that infants need affectionate touch and affirmative attention as much as they need sunshine and food. When given food, but not affection and affirmation, they languish and have lasting detrimental psychological and physical effects.

The need for happy, healthy relationships does not stop at infancy, though such are truly formative years when it's absolutely essential. This basic need goes on for all our lives, even up to our last moments. We humans survive and thrive when we can give to others, and receive back from them, honest reassurance that our existence matters in the form of their affection and appreciation.

Marilyn

As a health care chaplain, and in particular a hospice chaplain, I cannot stress how true it is that even unto our dying moments, perhaps most in those moments, we need gentle touch, reassuring words, soothing tones and loving eye contact. I have seen it in their expressions, how much they appreciate being acknowledged as "still one of us, the living," in these ways.

Becoming our own best friend, through positive self-reflection and affirming self-talk rather than harsh self-recrimination is an effective way to generate the energy we need as we devise solutions.

"Friends don't let friends drive drunk," can be translated here to, "Best friends don't let themselves accept negative self-talk as pronouncements from on high." When you feel the urge to talk yourself down, take the keys from your negative mind and don't get in that self-berating car that will drive you down the road to a self-inflicted toxic state of mind highway exit.

The need for happy, healthy relationships does not stop at infancy, though such are truly formative years when it's absolutely essential. This basic need goes on for all our lives, even up to our last moments. We humans survive and thrive when we can give to others, and receive back from them, honest reassurance that our existence matters in the form of their affection and appreciation.

Instead, stay at home or in your office for 20 minutes with the Miracle Question, imagining your life as you want to live it, being the person you truly desire to be. Go spelunking for Exceptions and Examples. Do some Sudoku math with Evaluating.

Do something different from putting yourself down and wallowing around yet again in Problem Expert thinking.

When you've come up with a fun solution step that you know you're very likely to do, give yourself back the keys as you are probably now "sober" (solution oriented) enough to drive. And then, as we like to say, "Never leave home without your positive self-regarding BFF!

12. Don't Sweat the Detours

Why backsliding doesn't mean you're going to hell ... SERIOUSLY

Results vary. 'Tis true. We can't get around the fact that some of us are self-starters and others need a bit of handholding along the way. In the case of the co-authors, Karen is the former and Marilyn is the latter. By the way, neither one is better than the other. In fact, these tendencies indicate to us the strengths that we bring to any of our endeavors.

Self-starters get out of the gate fast, but over time discover they could use some help in slowing down and taking care of necessary details (Oh, those details!) On the other hand, those who need some support at first later stoke their creative fires and off they go all on their own!

What we *all* do is stray from whatever solution course we set for ourselves. There are all sorts of reasons why.

We like lists, so we have to give you at least one in this book. This one delineates why we our results tend to vary:

1) We set the solutions strategies too far ahead.

Keeping your solutions to the present is the better way to go. Don't try to make a 5-year plan for your solutions. It rarely worked for Russia's economy, and is not any more likely to work for you. (Setting 5-year goals is fine–but they serve a different purpose than Matrix solution steps).

2) We set the solution-goal too high.

Problems hurt. We want them gone, and now, not later. We understand. We feel the same. But, this is a "get real" program. The best way to get rid of a problem is to practice a solution, one small doable step at a time. Self-starters sometimes overestimate their first step and after an initial failure declare the project defunct. Hand-holders sometimes underestimate their capacity to take that first step and procrastinate … forever.

3) We become impatient with ourselves.

We like fast results. It is what drives our current medical model. Have a headache? Take a pill. You could drink water, eat a banana and get some rest. But, that takes time.

Solutions also take time, but not as long as you might think. Some problems have been with us for years. How can they possibly go away overnight? They usually don't, but what can go away, and fairly quickly is problem oriented thinking.

Once we release ourselves from having to know everything about a problem, and turn toward finding solutions, doing something different, recalling our past in a positive perspective, the problem does start to change.

Sometimes small changes are all that we get, but they are better than no change at all. Sometimes we get huge changes, but then have to contend with what all that does to ourselves and our relationships.

Either way, it all takes time. Don't force solutions, please. That only makes for another problem at that point. Yes, do focus on solutions, but try them on for size, adjust them, alter them, and sometimes give them away to the thrift store so you have room in our closet for new ones.

4) We get lulled into complacency.

We sometimes think, after accomplishing a few successful solution steps, "That's the end of *that*." Unfortunately, old habits die hard. Ask those with serious issues who need AA support for example. They know full well that while an old habit may fade, it lingers just around the corner in the dark and needs a steady eye on it at all times.

It would be the very, very rare occasion that we devise a solution step that makes the problem disappear once and for all. It's always a process.

Backsliding, or returning to old behaviors that keep the problem alive in our lives is *normal*. It would be the very, very rare occasion that we devise a solution step that makes the problem disappear once and for all. It's always a process.

When you find yourself up to your keister in the muck of a problem, raking it back and forth, again and again in your mind and you realize you're wallowing around in a Problem Expert mode again–that's wonderful!

What?! That's right. Knowing that you *know* you're back into an old habit is a good thing. Now, you can do something different. See how handily that works?

You really have come a long way, baby! After all, you've been through brain freeze, the Principles, Rules of Thumb and the Matrix. Gotcha! There's no going back.

So, just hop onto your solutions wagon and keep going. You might have a long way to go, but don't ever forget just how far, far, far you have already come.

13. How to Get More From What You've Already Got

PLAY

So you want more and for less? Join the human race! Whether you realize it or not, you really do have some neat stuff in your back pocket, gems and jewels, real diamonds in the rough, that you may have forgotten about, or discounted as to be of little use. We have shown you where to find them using the Matrix.

Now we want to go over 3 things you can do to leverage your existing capacities to get more out of what you already have and who you already are!

Wall Street likes to talk about leveraged buyouts, operating leverage, leverage ratios or simply techniques that amplify investor profits or losses. We like to talk about ways to amplify your gains (and losses of the not so helpful stuff) in your everyday life.

Here we want to give you some bonus tips (not advice, just little add-ons to enhance your program). This is our way of giving you more for less, because though we could put all this stuff into another book, why make you wait, and pay more to boot? (We're not that greedy, and also, honestly, it's hard to write a good book. We're not sure when we'll produce another one in this genre, so we're giving it all to you now!).

First of all, we want to emphasize the importance of **PLAY!** We really mean it. PLAY, PLAY, PLAY!

Karen devised the whole thing about PLAY because she had students like Marilyn who are convinced they lack the genetic material that lends them to find the FUN!

There are studies about the importance of play in childhood. Playing is essential to growth, development, enjoyment and vitality! But for some reason, perhaps because we don't want to appear silly in the serious adult world, the value of play is often lost on us. Not always, but sadly all too often.

Of course, play is a context-appropriate activity, although even a very serious moment can incorporate play.

Marilyn

As a hospice chaplain, I'm often in serious scenarios. What's more serious than someone dying? Even so, if it's appropriate, I allow for some play in certain situations. Here's an example. Do note that this story occurred after rapport had been established over time with the patient and his loved ones.

It was the day before a patient died and he knew his time was near. His loving wife of more than 60 years was quite tearful while she held his hand at bedside. I sat with her and asked her to share one of her fondest memories with him. She began to recount a story of a trip they took to a neighboring state. At one point, her frail husband lifted his hand and said, "No, that's not how it happened."

She smiled. I looked over at her husband and gently teased him. "You're almost ready to die and you still have to correct her?" He looked at his spouse and grinned. "Yep" he whispered.

She was also grinning. A few of the adult children had entered the room and they said, "They've been correcting each other for decades. Why should they stop now?" When I met them later at a memorial service, they said this would remain a new, fond, forever memory for all the family.

Sure, there are times to be serious and the story above does not mean the chaplain is always at play. But, there is the obvious value of play—enjoying a game with family and friends, slowing down enough to engage in a humorous moment with a colleague over coffee, talking to a lizard in the back yard, watching humming birds flit around a feeder, or taking a weekend hike to enjoy some fresh air.

At the risk of repeating ourselves since we did introduce this earlier, we want to remind you of the potency of PLAY. This particular form of PLAY may be the "getting you out of a tough spot more easily" kind of play rather than the kind of play that is simply fun. But then we like to consider less stress and less problems as being in the "fun" category because it can make you smile, ever so quietly to yourself!

Because problems often show up as unexpected challenges in the midst of important events, when you don't have time to methodically go through the lines of inquiry, we want you to have this tool at your fingertips. And it helps to have taken it through a few practice runs so you are ready to use it when you really need it!

This "little tool" helps you get through those moments when a problem raises its ugly head so you are not beaten by it. Here we go again. Just skip these few lines if they are already second nature for you.

You will see that we have used it in slightly different ways already in the book, and we encourage you to use it any way that works for you. What is important is that you start a pattern of intentional actions when problems, stress or difficulties arise and grow your confidence and mastery!

Pause (and breathe, taking in longer-than-usual, slow breaths all the way down so your stomach extends, not just so your shoulders move);

Lean in (accept that you're in the mucky muck again, rather than deny or resist it, and then think of one small thing you can do differently, just one small thing...);

Adapt to this small change (seek feedback and when you get it, non-defensively respond to it as useful information for what to do next, and next, and next);

enjo**Y**—Celebrate that you're doing this, for yourself and for those you care about!

A lot of solutions focusing is discovering who you more truly are and what you really want, all the while taking inventive little steps toward that new reality. In fact, those very steps are the new reality. So, keep taking them!

All that we're saying here is that you are allowed to celebrate what you're discovering about yourself. You have the resilience and the resources within you to solve your problems. Does that mean you don't see a doctor when you need one? *No!*

If you need a psychologist for a while, by all means, see one. If you need to attend a support group, by all means, attend one on a regular basis and keep close tabs with your sponsor. If you need to see a pastoral or a loss/grief counselor, then by all means find these persons and let them help you get on with your life.

In all that while, you can use solutions focusing, adding the Matrix approach to all these other interventions. Self-help is the portion of changes you can make in your life, on your own.

PLAY allows us to engage the process fully. We can test things out, do things we haven't done before. If we make a mistake, we say, "Oops" and stop doing that. We then focus on the actions that do work, and we do them more often.

Solutions Coaching

Here, we are going to introduce the concept of a solutions coach. This is not the same as a therapist or counselor. You are the main player in this relationship. Like any athlete, you do most of the work, and deserve most of the accolades when the victories come.

However, the reality is that we are sometimes so close to the problem that we just can't see it clearly any more. In Australia there are tough little scrub bushes that grow like weeds in the fields. You can spend all day clearing them out, but after a while, you miss one or two as you go through the paddock.

The next day, you go back to the field, and there are still dozens left even though you cleared hundreds of them out. You were certain there were none left, but there they are. What happened? Did all those plants grow overnight? Nope. You really could no longer see them anymore.

Aussies call this effect, "burr blind."

This is where the value of an experienced solutions coach comes in. This is why so many high performers do seek out mentors and coaches, not because mentors and coaches know everything, but because they know the process and can support us as we maneuver through a new way of thinking, feeling and being.

Coaches are not friends, though they are usually very friendly people. Neither are they family members or colleagues at work. This gives them, and you, a good professional working relationship that allows you to be honest about your process. That's their main interest, that you are using the Matrix in as efficient and effective manner as is possible for you.

In short we are talking about creating a partnership that liberates your creativity so you can produce your finest work: becoming the person you truly want to be.

To find a solutions coach, go to the following website: http://www.TheSolutionRevolution.co or search for someone in your area who specializes in some "solution focused" coaching.

The Buddy System

Getting a buddy to work with you as you begin to understand and use the Solutions Mastery System is not quite the same boost as obtaining a coach, but it is a good way to get started and keep going, so long as you have chosen a fairly trustworthy buddy.

Having a buddy can help keep you on track and noticing things that you may not otherwise observe. So, if coaching does not feel quite right at the beginning (though it may later on if you get the yen for greater results at a faster pace), get out there and find a buddy.

Get a friend to do this work with you. You will be delighted with how this can deepen and expand an already good friendship. If you can't find someone you already know to buddy up with, then consider finding one through a Bootcamp startup course.

Or, you can join in a Mastermind Group of new and experienced Matrix users. The point is, find someone you can consider your buddy in this work, who will remind you when you are wallowing, to notice the things you do well when you forget and start to DAG out a little. You can help and be helped enormously by a buddy.

To find out more about the Bootcamp startup course or when the next Mastermind will start, go to the website: http://www.TheSolutionRevolution.co.

Mastermind Groups

Last, but very much not least, we want to mention the benefits and advantages of networking, connecting and making friendships with others who are as focused as you are, on strengthening their capacity as innovators and change-agents.

In today's global community, Mastermind Groups allow small groups of like-minded individuals to develop themselves or their businesses and careers by working together, in a supportive environment, usually over the Internet.

These groups serve as an encouraging environment and spark each member's creativity There is room for constructive critiquing, though not negative criticism—there is a vast difference.

We are social animals, to put it in biological terms. Working with a small community or team of people to help us hone our skills, and even wrestle together on some of our tougher issues, all the while engaging, inspiring and providing one another with new connections, can be priceless.

We are social animals, to put it in biological terms. Working with a small community or team of people to help us hone our skills, and even wrestle together on some of our tougher issues, all the while engaging, inspiring and providing one another with new connections, can be priceless.

A Mastermind Group might be right for you if you are seeking any of the following:

Community: Being part of an exclusive community where the others need you as much as you need them, so quality of experience is crucial to all.

Somewhere to Turn: "Being alone" can be one of the most stultifying feelings, but in a Mastermind Group, all the members provide valuable insights and perspectives and other life-changing gifts.

Collaboration: Being social animals, when we work as a group, it is easier to identify and then deal with real (and not just perceived) crises. Collaboration increases the likelihood of finding and making the connections we really need to flourish.

New Learning: Mastermind Groups usually involve persons from different backgrounds, industries and life experiences, so there is an enormous opportunity to learn and broaden ourselves. Plus, it's almost certain that someone in your Mastermind Group will have a unique angle on your sticking point (and you on theirs). We might successfully hide such points from ourselves, but there is potential for others to help you see them to through your conversations and meetings.

Think Even Bigger: Mastermind Groups can definitely facilitate this to happen. When you are surrounded by people contending with and constructing amazing innovations, you cannot help but think bigger and expand your horizons. Sometimes, you will find yourself sharing your amazing innovations. Mastermind Groups affirm who we are by allowing others to hear what we have to say, and receiving from them the compliments that are due to us.

Personal and Professional Growth: Personal and professional growth is simply what happens in a Mastermind Group, and it is done with all the benefits (but none of the cronyism) of a good-old boys networks.

Why none of the cronyism? A Mastermind Group is moderated by an experienced Solutions Coach.

Their purpose is to keep the conversation flowing, making sure that all participants are affirmed for their input. They serve the purpose of allowing for creative thoughts to emerge, even the ones that seem too far out of the field to be applied.

Such may or may not be the case, but the point is that the Mastermind Group is about seeking new ways to approach old, stuck-in-the-muck problems. Sometimes a crazy idea that makes everyone laugh also has a hidden grain of real truth, and in noticing that, some of the best "realistic" ideas can come out.

Find out about our Mastermind Groups at: http://www.TheSolutionRevolution.co, or simply put what you learned here to work in one of your other mastermind groups.

So long, but not farewell

Our parting words are simple. We want to thank you for reading this far, even if you turned to this page and read it first.

We want to encourage you to explore solutions focusing as a new way to approach your life. And, we simply want to say that we love you. We do. We can't help it. You are seeking to better yourself. You are reading this book.

You remind us of how we started this journey, how far we've come and how much FUN! it has been, even though there were hard times (more than a few). You remind us that there is still a ways to go, and so, even more revelations, discoveries and FUN! to be had!

All that is truly loveable.

We are a lot like you. We understand your desire to improve your life, to live in a way that is authentic, compassionate, creative, and, as we've said in so many ways, *more fun* than dwelling on problems and the sorrows they burden us with.

Life is short. It should be filled as much as possible with happiness. We know that you can't make every minute happy, but you can certainly create better relationships, starting with the one you have with yourself where joy is allowed to creep into, no, overwhelmingly fill up the center of it.

So yes, we do hope this little book helps you "get real," "get happy" and most of all, get you to where you want to be, the person you want others to know and love for who you really and truly are.

All the best in your endeavor,
Dr. Karen Judd Smith
Chaplain Marilyn Morris

Part V. Resources

Glossary

bootcamp The "CHANGE !T UP Bootcamp" is the online training program designed specifically to take you by the hand and personally walk you through the Solutions Mastery Matrix so you start building solutions without feeling like you have to become someone else to make a big difference in your life. Check the site for more information: http://TheSolutionRevolution.co.

In just a few weeks, you walk away with:

- Your own Solutions Building System that works *for* you, where you are today
- The know-how needed to leverage what you *do* know and stop you from letting what you *don't* know drag you down
- Knowing what to do in the first 5-15 seconds when you get triggered by the perplexing effects of an old (or brand new) problem
- How to be kind to yourself *and* keep on making significant progress becoming who you really want to be and toward the goals you really want to achieve
- Two secrets to getting yourself unstuck fast when you feel you are knee deep in Mississippi mud and can't make that first step forward

- The exact questions to ask yourself to plumb the hidden riches of your life
- A new found self-confidence that comes with knowing what to do whenever trouble arises

doom and gloom loop (DAG loop): This is the "take it with you pity party" that many people identify in others as Eeyore-like characters. Many know the donkey in A.A. Milne's Winnie the Pooh:

"Good morning, Pooh Bear," said Eeyore gloomily. "If it is a good morning," he said. "Which I doubt," said he.

You may recognize it in yourself as a partly noble barrier, protecting you from disappointment. But in the end, it is an unconscious addiction to gloomy outcomes. An almost invisible self-fulfilling prophesy of sorts, because "acceptance" of this view means you have adopted certain filters through which you are viewing that part of your life.

The DAG loop is easily remedied by noticing. When you notice you have entered this loop, just think "Hah! DAG-1, JS-2" And for 2 minutes think about the outcomes you *want*. Anything, but the gloom and pain you may be using as the "protection" that is undermining your preferred life!

Plus another bit of Aussie insight for you. Dag is a slang term that is often used as an affectionate insult. Yes, this may be news to many Americans, but to Aussies, insults are often a form of affection! Go figure.

Back to dags—A dag refers to being unfashionable, eccentric or fool-like and has no class connotations. And we do have to add, that its literal meaning is "a dung-caked lock of wool around the hindquarters of a sheep, a daglock." These (or the potential for them) are why sheep are crutched. It is this part of the meaning of dag that should motivate you the most to stay away from the DAG loop. It's unhealthy at best!

fun: An essential component of any new endeavor that helps you keep working on it even through the tough spots (since when do they never happen?!). In fact, it is mandated by Karen to be a part of any successful solution.

iterative: A term more often used in common language now that we are increasingly surrounded by computational processes and so notice them at work in our lives as well. Daily habits are iterative. Practicing getting goals in basketball or any sport is iterative. When infused with the fun of success, no matter how large or small, building iterative skills is hard to resist!

The role of iterative development is evident in agile project management (SCRUM), curriculum design methods such as SAM (Successive Approximation Model) and since the start of time as PLAY in human development.

JS2—The Jump Start 2-Minute: This is a simple stratagem for dealing with procrastination by giving yourself a white slate to play with for a brief period of time. Get your pen (or tool of trade) and immerse yourself for **just 2 minutes** in any endeavor (exercise, writing, homework, whatever) you think might spark you forward.

mastermind: Small groups of like-minded individuals who work together to develop themselves or their businesses and careers in a supportive environment, often over the Internet, that sparks one another's creativity and helps with accountability and synergy.

For Pinky, the mastermind is the Brain.

play: Play is an essential part of human development. While it is voluntary, play is intrinsically motivated by and associated with pleasure and enjoyment. For adults and children alike—OK, adults use the grown-up word "recreation"—but play can be a delightful doorway to cognitive, social and physical development.

PLAY: A social technology that leverages some well known practical benefits of deep breathing (more benefits available when some of the practical sides of transilience a lá Karen are explored, but we don't go there in this book).

Pause (breathe deeply to reconnect with your body)
Lean in (Don't fight the moment. Do take the opportunity to Look for **exceptions** and **examples**)
Adapt (now aware of Exceptions & Examples, Adapt what you know works, to help your current way forward)
EnjoY!—(celebrate what you have achieved, no matter how small)!

principles at play: These are principles like any other. They are on the immutable side, not things that you can negotiate (perhaps unless you are a god or a demi-god). What is helpful about these particular ones is that they provide insight useful when we are struggling with some issue in our lives. They help us know what cannot be changed so we can then focus on something that we can impact.

What's even better yet about principles is that when we know them, they can become a kind of useful tool for us. They enable us to do things that, without knowledge of them, we are simply unable to intentionally accomplish.

Awareness and use of principles is power.

Here's a quick list of the principles at play and a downloadable printout, should you like to have these somewhere to ponder some time:

1) Change is always happening.
2) Small changes accumulate into bigger changes.
3) Change in our own sphere of influence naturally (and inexorably) affects change in others.
4) You invest in what you create.
5) You are the expert of your life.
6) You have the resources and resilience.
7) You want to get better and are doing the best you can.
8) You do not need to know anything about a problem in order to create an effective solution for it.
9) Exceptions indicate solutions.
10) The simplest and least invasive approach is usually the best medicine.

Download the pdf here: http://goo.gl/ZudGe0

problem: A matter or situation regarded as unwelcome or harmful and needing to be dealt with and overcome. Problems in our lives usually interfere with our emotional or physical health, our relationships, work productivity and our happiness.

Problems can also be a means for us to transform our lives. They point out the areas of our lives that are limiting us and in this light, are wonderfully helpful, because now, with the Solutions Matrix in hand, you can Change It Up, create a solution and end up in a far better place than without you having encountered that problem!

Yes, problems can really help us out, that is when you know what to do with them! Go all in and PLAY as you JS2 the Matrix!

Problem Expert: A person who knows all about a problem, as to who caused it, why it happened in the first, second and third place, why it is so big that it is really not solvable, especially because it is so sticky and the ones who caused it will never change.

Further, they have an abundance of proof: old conversations reiterated daily; all the books they've read on the problem; lists of facts as to how it is typical for this day and age; umpteen reasons why the problem simply won't go away; rehashed memories of past experiences from both recent and distant occurrences; proof of how the problem originated and who all remains responsible for it still happening. They are exceptionally good at showing how the problem is intractable and that there is little to nothing that can really be done about it.

rules of thumb: This is the list of preferred self-talk we would like you to use. They are based upon the Principles at Play and you might think of them as your helpful Minions, there to help you all the way to your solutions!

Here is the list:
1) Start at the beginning and not at the end.
2) If it is working, do more of it.
3) If it isn't working, try something else.

4) Keep it Simple.
5) Focus on strengths and resources, not on weaknesses and deficits.
6) Look forward, not back.
7) No single approach works for everyone.
8) Solutions focusing is not solutions forcing.
9) Complaining about others never creates solutions.
10) Look for the FUN!

Download a pdf version of the list to print out here: http://goo.gl/ZudGe0

solution: The state of being solved; the act of solving a problem or question. The way we look at "solutions" in this book is as a creative process that we engage in as the optimal way to resolve the predicament of having a problem or complaint.

the Solutions Matrix (the Matrix): A matrix of 5 questions or lines of inquiry that when used together, or even alone, get the user started on a solution focused" approach to problem solving.

Here it is again. You can also download a copy to print out and put in your pocket from here: http://goo.gl/R9yCBt

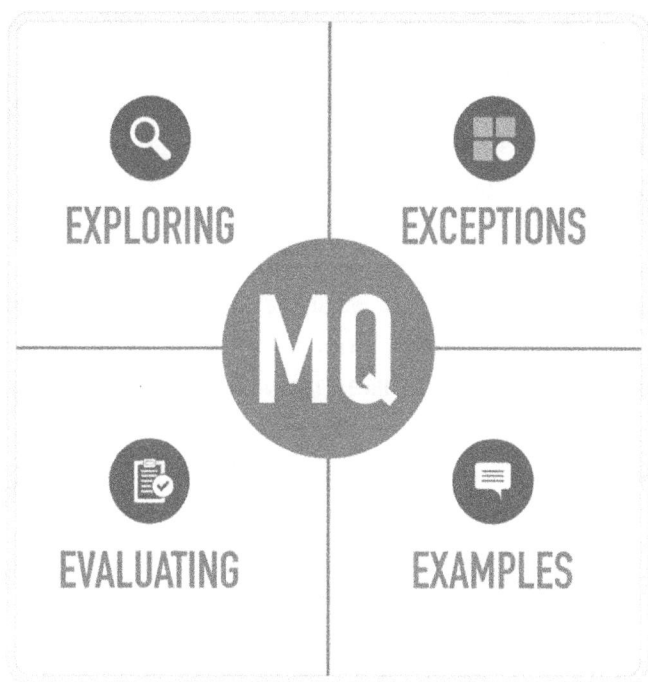

EXPLORING   EXCEPTIONS

MQ

EVALUATING   EXAMPLES

Solutions Focused Brief Therapy (SFBT): A goal oriented form of therapy targeting the building of desired outcomes as a solution rather than focusing on the symptoms or issues that brought someone to therapy. This technique emphasizes present and future circumstances and desires over past experiences.

Solutions Master: One who actively engages in a creative process as their response to problems rather than wasting time reliving or reinvigorating the conditions that created the problem in the first place. The solutions master knows they have limited time and energy in their life and choose to use those precious resources constructing solutions rather than revivifying problems.

Solutions Mastery System: This includes the Solutions Matrix and the understanding of the principles at play in our lives that are relevant to the solutions building process and the helpful rules of thumb that are used as reminders.

SRTs—Solutions Rules of Thumb: These are the friendly reminders that we would rather you have rattling around in your head than other common thoughts such as: "It's no use." "It's always like that with him/her." "Problems are hard." "The problem is just too complicated." "I'm not enough." "It's always this way." "It doesn't matter what I do." "Nothing ever works." "It's too hard." "No one ever listens." "Woe is me." Yes, having Rules of Thumb in your head like, "I have the necessary resources and resilience that I need," is really much better, don't you think?

transilience:
1. the capacity to leap or pass from one thing or state to another
2. the capacity to break through
3. the ability of a person to initiate intentional change.

In the context of this work, transilience is our capacity for change that builds especially when we focus on constructing solutions that draw upon the oft forgotten or underestimated successes in our own life and experience.

While transilience is barely mentioned by name in this book, Karen views it as the underlying capacity that fuels and strengthens our breakthroughs and transformations. Others may more generally refer to this capacity as: creativity, ingenuity, inventiveness, resourcefulness, genius, wisdom, etc.

Books

These are some of our favorite Solutions Building, Change Leadership, Iterative Development Books.

Allen, Michael W, and Richard H. Sites. Leaving Addie for Sam: An Agile Model for Developing the Best Learning Experiences. Alexandria, Va.: American Society for Training and Development, 2012. Print.

Berg, Insoo K, and Peter Szabó. Brief Coaching for Lasting Solutions. New York: W.W. Norton, 2005. Print.

Berg, Insoo K, and Therese Steiner. Children's Solution Work. New York: Norton, 2003. Print.

De, Shazer S, Yvonne M. Dolan, and Harry Korman. More Than Miracles: The State of the Art of Solution-focused Brief Therapy, New York: Haworth Press, 2007. Print.

De, Shazer S. Clues: Investigating Solutions in Brief Therapy. New York: W.W. Norton, 1988. Print.

De, Shazer S. Words Were Originally Magic. New York: W.W. Norton, 1994. Print.

De, Shazer S. Keys to Solution in Brief Therapy. New York: W.W. Norton, 1985. Print.

De, Shazer S. Putting Difference To Work. New York: Norton, 1991. Print.

Hasher, Lynn, David Goldstein, and Thomas Toppino. "Frequency and the Conference of Referential Validity." *Journal of Verbal Learning and Verbal Behavior.* 16.1 (1977): 107-112. Print. *More information about the "Illusory Truth Effect"*

Kotter, John P. A Sense of Urgency. Boston, Mass: Harvard Business Press, 2008. Print.

Kotter, John P. Leading Change. Boston, Mass: Harvard Business School Press, 1996. Print.

Kotter, John P, and Lorne A. Whitehead. Buy-in: Saving Your Good Idea from Getting Shot Down. Boston, Mass: Harvard Business Review Press, 2010. Print.

Miller, Scott D, and Insoo K. Berg. The Miracle Method: A Radically New Approach to Problem Drinking. New York: W.W. Norton, 1995. Print.

Walter, John L, and Jane E. Peller. Becoming Solution-Focused in Brief Therapy. New York: Brunner/Mazel, 1992. Print.

Miscellaneous
Videos, Links & Resources

Agile e-Learning Development Process
http://www.alleninteractions.com/sam-process.

Flashbulb Memories: Why do we remember dramatic
events so vividly?
An article: http://goo.gl/GyuAOV.

Reading is believing: The truth effect and source
credibility.
A pdf: http://goo.gl/COfjD1.

Unconscious Processing:
An extended abstract on the research: http://goo.gl/a043fF.

Remembering is Believing: Illusion of Truth Effect
https://vimeo.com/71671086.

Your Body Language Shapes Who You Are
A TED video with Amy Cuddy.
https://goo.gl/vmpbuC

Negativity Bias, Negativity Dominance, and Contagion
Paul Rozin and Edward B. Royzman
http://goo.gl/i5qY5Z

Solut!ons Opportunities

CHANGE !T UP: *The Solutions Mastery Bootcamp*
http://TheSolutionRevolution.co/bootcamp/.

Transilience: *The Innovation and Influence Mastermind*
http://TheSolutionRevolution.co/transilience/.

A Solutions Matrix Printout:
Download a pdf from this url to print out and put in your
pocket: http://goo.gl/R9yCBt.

Solutions Principles At Play & Rules of Thumb PDF:
http://goo.gl/ZudGe0

About the Authors

Karen Judd Smith has been dubbed a Queen of Innovation with regard to her simple yet effective approach to breakthrough, innovation and action. In recent years her **Solutions Mastery System**, a "GPS for successful living," has helped people get unstuck and driving the changes they seek.

She continues her work with international organizations, addressing issues central to humanity's future, and predicts that frameworks such as the *Solutions Matrix* will help structure the kind of global dialogues needed to successfully address existential risks like superintelligence.

For more information visit: http://www.KarenJuddSmith.com.

Marilyn Morris, known as "The Singing Chaplain," is a theologian and board certified chaplain, who, since 2000, has served thousands of patients and their loved ones, providing comfort and guidance as they faced emergency crises, approached end of life, and suffered with loss and grief. Based on personal experience with the Solutions Mastery System she envisions it will unleash creative energies desperately needed in our conflicted problem oriented world.

For more information: http://www.TheSingingChaplain.com.